SIBURAPHA

BEHIND THE PAINTING

AND OTHER STORIES

Translated from the Thai and introduced by

DAVID SMYTH

 Silkworm Books

ข้างหลังภาพ โดย ศรีบูรพา
© 1954 by Kulap Saipradit
English translation © 1995 by David Smyth

All rights reserved. No part of this publication may be reproduced, stored in a retrieval system, or transmitted, in any form or by any means, electronic, mechanical, photocopying, recording or otherwise, without the prior permission in writing of the publisher.

ISBN 978-974-7551-14-3

First published in Thailand in 2000 by
Silkworm Books
6 Sukkasem Road, Suthep, Chiang Mai, Thailand
E-mail: info@silkwormbooks.com
www.silkwormbooks.com

Cover design by Trasvin Jittidecharak
Cover graphic by Umaphon Soetphannuek
Set in 11 pt. Garamond by Silk Type

CONTENTS

3

INTRODUCTION

Behind the Painting is widely regarded as one of the best-written novels in the Thai language. The first twelve chapters were originally serialized in the daily newspaper *Prachachat* between December 1937 and January 1938, and the complete novel subsequently published as a volume later that same year. Since then, it has been reprinted on almost forty occasions, with the total number of copies printed over the years being close to one hundred thousand; it is studied in Thai secondary schools, has been translated into Japanese and Chinese, and was made into a film in the early 1980s.

The story unfolds in flashback and is narrated by Nopphon, a Thai student studying in Japan. It tells of his youthful infatuation with Mom Ratchawong Kirati, an older woman, visiting the country with her husband. Her return to Thailand and the passage of time soon cool his ardor; only some years later, after he has returned home, does he learn from the dying Mom Ratchawong Kirati that his original feelings for her had been reciprocated. Within this framework, Siburapha skillfully evokes the erotic undercurrent of frustrated sexuality and the sense of conspiracy that soon permeate relations between Nopphon and Mom Ratchawong Kirati, yet "with such delicacy," according to the highly respected critic, M.L. Bunlua Thepyasuwan, "that it did not appear morally wrong."

Thai critics have admired the work both for its artistic and technical qualities, its particular merits being seen to lie in the characterization, the careful construction of the plot, with its subtle ironies, the exotic setting and "the poetic and evocative" use of language. In the character of Mom Ratchawong Kirati, the author portrays something of the stifling existence endured by a certain class of women, though the fears she voices about ageing, the frailty of men's love, and the trap of a joyless marriage, are universally understood. Nopphon's character emerges indirectly and as a result is often overlooked. This is an unfortunate omission, because the novel is as much about a young man's awaken-ing to the frailty of his emotions as the tragic circumstances of Mom Ratchawong Kirati's life. And as with any well-written "confessional novel," the reader is ultimately left to ponder the credibility of the narrator's account of events.

What sets *Behind the Painting* apart from Siburapha's earlier novels and many other tragic love stories of the period, is the author's attempt to deal with characters and their emotions with a degree of realism and honesty not always compatible with the conventions of the genre. Had he written the novel ten years earlier, one can well imagine that Mom Ratchawong Kirati's husband, Chao Khun, would have been portrayed as a melo-dramatic villain in order to justify her behavior, and that Nopphon's passion would have been fueled to unbearable intensity by the long separation, or at the very least, would have been rekindled in the final scene. As it is, Chao Khun is a perfect-ly harmless creature, and it is through Mom Ratchawong Kirati's initially subtle, but subsequently grotesquely blunt references to her husband's inadequacies that the reader is drawn in to sympathizing with her plight, scarcely noticing that the age gap that separates her from her apparently elderly husband is identical to that between her and Nopphon. And for Nopphon, the letter-writing, which initially offers such emotional sustenance, soon becomes an irksome duty and his subsequent clumsy attempts to spare her feelings are characterized by an authentic mixture of embarrassment, self-deception, and emotional numbness.

While most Thai critics have tended to see *Behind the Painting* as a straightforward love story, Udom Sisuwan, a prominent journalist, literary critic, and later high-ranking member of the Communist Party of Thailand, offered a rather more politicized interpretation of the novel, in which he saw the protaganists as symbols of their respective classes. "The tragedy of Mom Ratchawong Kirati," he argued in an essay written in 1950, "amounts to a portrayal of the destruction of the upper class," while "the dishonesty of Nopphon is the dishonesty of the *compradore* capitalist class which flourished after the end of the absolute monarchy." Udom's essay was reprinted a number of times during the mid-1970s, and his interpretation of the novel is often echoed, almost certainly unwittingly, by textbook writers today. Udom's bold, but unsupported assertions, are perhaps best understood as an attempt to reconcile Siburapha's reputation as a "progressive" writer and social critic with the fact that this, his most popular novel, was a romance set among the élite.

The short stories *Those Kind of People*, *Lend Us a Hand*, and *The Awakening*, which first appeared between 1949 and 1952, stand in dramatic contrast to *Behind the Painting*, which appeared just over a decade earlier. In these and other stories written at the same time, Siburapha set out to fire the reader with anger and indignation at social and political injustice. He made ordinary working people the heroes of this fiction and the stories describe, often at considerable length, their cramped and smelly living conditions, their long hours of low-paid work, the ever-present threat of sickness and the inadequacy or inaccessibility of medical care. The plot invariably involves them in conflict with an exploiting class of petty-minded aristocrats, hard-nosed business-men or corrupt government officials, and as a result, they begin to question their former passive acceptance of the status quo. And since Siburapha had come to see it as the role of the writer to point the way forward rather than merely chronicle the plight of the underclass, the stories generally end on a deliberately positive note which implies that change is possible and that every individual has their part to play, no matter how small it may seem.

The appearance of these stories, and, indeed, Udom's essay on *Behind the Painting*, coincided with a brief period when the government relaxed restrictions on freedom of speech in order to gain Russian support for its application to the United Nations. One result was a sudden proliferation of radical publications, including the Communist Party of Thailand weekly, *Mahachon* ("The Masses"). This period of liberalization did not last long, however, and amid the worsening Cold War, Thailand adopted an increasingly virulent anti-communist stance. Siburapha was one of a number of intellectuals arrested in a government clamp-down on internal opposition in 1952 and sentenced to lengthy prison terms. When Field Marshal Sarit Thanarat seized power in 1958, heralding a "dark age" for Thai writers, such was the climate of fear that few dared to speak openly of Siburapha—now in self-imposed exile in China—for fear of being labeled a communist. While there was a major reprint of many of his early novels shortly after the death of Sarit in 1963, his later short stories remained out of circulation until the early 1970s, when student activist groups began sponsoring the publication of his and other radical writers' works. In fact, buy-ing, reading, or merely carrying around a copy of Siburapha's later short stories became a way of making a statement about one's political beliefs, while imitating the themes and tone of his work became the stock-in-trade of many aspiring young writers of the period.

Since the early 1970s these stories have been reprinted frequently, with *Lend Us a Hand* included in an anthology published by the Thai Writer's Association in 1985 to commemo-rate the centennial of the short story in Thailand. While the Western reader, unaccustomed to "committed literature" and unfamiliar with postwar Thai history, may well remain sceptical about the merits of Siburapha's later short stories, for many Thais who had grown up in a period of strict censorship, they were like a beacon in the dark, a defiant expression of their own idealism.

Siburapha is the pen-name of Kulap Saipradit. He was born in Bangkok on 31 March 1905 into a family of modest means. His interest in writing was awakened during his secondary education at the prestigious Thepsirin School. At this time prose fiction was still in its infancy in Thailand: the first translation of a Western novel, Marie Corelli's *Vendetta*, had appeared in 1900, while the first Thai novel, *Khwam Mai Phayabat* ("Non-Vendetta"), which parodied Corelli's work in its title, was published in 1915. The early 1920s saw a rapid increase in the number of magazines and journals, many of which not only openly solicited contributions from their readers, but actually depended upon them for survival. At first, the fiction pages of these magazines were filled with translations or adaptations of Western novels or pseudo-Western novels where the characters were given Western names. But by the mid-1920s the public's taste began to move towards stories with realistic Thai characters and settings.

It was against this background of a fundamental change in popular literary taste that Siburapha emerged as one of Thai-land's most popular novelists. His first full-length work, *Luk Phuchai* ("A Real Man"), appeared in October 1928 and proved an immediate success and the following year he launched a short-lived but highly regarded fortnightly magazine called *Suphap-burut* ("The Gentleman"). This, together with his own prolific output, which included four further novels and several short stories within the space of little more than twelve months, effectively secured his reputation both among the reading public and his fellow writers.

After the demise of *Suphapburut,* Siburapha became more involved in political journalism. By the age of thirty, he had edited several of Bangkok's most prominent daily newspapers, although his tenure at each was often brief due to his political views. One of his best-known novels of the period, *Songkhram Chiwit* ("The War of Life"), published in 1932 just before the coup that brought an end to the absolute monarchy, reflects his increasing preoccupation with social injustice. In May 1936 Siburapha went to Japan for a year to study the Japanese news-paper industry, that country providing the setting for his most famous and stylistically most accomplished novel, *Khang Lang Phap* ("Behind the Painting").

Not long after his return to Thailand, Siburapha was given the backing to launch a new daily paper, which like his first successful venture of a decade earlier, included the name *Suphapburut* in its title. This was one of a small number of newspapers to adopt a consistently critical stance towards the policies of the Phibun government in the late 1930s. On a number of occasions Siburapha's articles aroused the ire of the government and in 1942 he was imprisoned for three months.

In 1947 Siburapha and his wife traveled to Australia to study the newspaper industry there. Returning in 1949, he began to write prolifically once again and to participate in public debates and seminars on such subjects as the social responsibility of the artist, the status of women, press censorship, and world peace. He became deputy chairman of the Thai chapter of the inter-national "Peace Movement," an organization set up in the late 1940s to campaign for the preservation of peace and nuclear disarmament, but viewed in the West as merely a front for communist propaganda. The movement sought to bring an end to the Korean War by a global mobilization of popular support through the worldwide collection of signatures on peace petitions. In Thailand, the government attacked the Peace Movement through the press by emphasizing its communist links, but found a pretext for more decisive action when Siburapha led a group of members of the peace committee, writers, journalists, and students on a much publicized trip to the northeastern provinces of Surin, Sisaket, and Khon Kaen in October 1952 to distribute blankets and medical supplies to victims of the recent floods. The government viewed Sibura-pha's Northeast mission as a deliberate challenge to its authority and an attempt to stir up hostility in a region that had long been politically sensitive for Bangkok-based administrations. Siburapha was arrested on 10 November 1952, the day after his return to Bangkok in part of a major swoop on internal opposi-tion. Half of the one hundred or so arrested were quickly released, but it was not until 15 March 1955 that the court delivered its verdict on the remainder. All except five were found guilty and most, including Siburapha, were sentenced to twenty years imprisonment, subsequently reduced by one third, in accordance with Thai custom, for their "helpful" testimony. Following an amnesty to commemorate the twenty-fifth centen-nial of the Buddha's birth, Siburapha was released on 20 February 1957, having spent a total of four years, three months, and ten days in prison. While in prison, Siburapha was far from idle, lecturing fellow inmates on politics, publishing articles on Buddhism, and completing the first part of the epic novel, *Lae Pai Khang Na* ("Look Forward"), which set out to provide a panoramic view of Thai history from the last days of the absolute monarchy.

In October 1957, some months after his release, Siburapha was invited to visit Russia to join celebrations to commemorate the fortieth anniversary of the revolution. The following September he led a delegation of twelve writers and journalists to the People's Republic of China at the invitation of the Chinese National Cultural Association. While in Beijing, he learned that Field Marshal Sarit Thanarat had seized power in Thailand in a military coup, and that fellow delegation members, who had returned earlier, had been arrested at Don Muang airport on charges of communism. Siburapha therefore decided to remain in China rather than return to certain imprisonment. He died in Beijing of heart and lung disease on 16 June 1974, aged sixty-nine, the last sixteen years of his life spent in exile.

Virtually a non-person during the oppressive Sarit regime (1958–63) when literary scholars dared not make any reference to him, Siburapha is today rightly regarded as one of the most significant figures in modern Thai literature. Many of his works have been reprinted, some have been filmed for television and cinema, a foundation and prestigious annual literary prize has been established in his name, a new literary magazine, also bearing his name, has appeared, and even a street in Bangkok has recently been named after him. This resurrection of Siburapha's name and the growth of his reputation is in itself an interesting reflection of political change and development in Thailand over the last twenty-five years.

BEHIND THE PAINTING

It was not until two days after I had hung the picture up in my study that Pari noticed it. She did not show much reaction, other than to pause and look closely at it for a moment, before turning to me and asking, "Where is it, this Mitake?" I was a little startled, but Pari did not notice.

"It's a lovely area of countryside outside Tokyo. People living in Tokyo often go there on Sundays."

"Oh, so you bought it in Tokyo, then?"

I buried my head in the book I had been reading when Pari entered the room.

"No, a friend of mine did it for me."

I felt uneasy about the way my voice had sounded, because it resembled that of an actor speaking in guarded fashion on stage.

"That's what I thought. It would have been a bit strange if you'd had to buy it, because it's very ordinary. But then while I don't see anything very special about it, it may just be that I'm not up to appreciating its merits."

"If you look at watercolors like this from close up, you might not appreciate them, but viewed from a little further back, you might have a different opinion."

Pari showed no inclination to do as I had suggested, nor to ask any more questions. I was glad. The painting was mounted in a jet black frame and hung on the wall immediately opposite my desk. When I sat down to work, it was behind me. I had thought of hanging it directly in front of me, so that I could see it whenever I looked up. But later, I changed my mind, being quite certain that if I were to follow through with my original idea, the painting would profoundly disturb my peace of mind.

In actual fact, Pari was not far wrong in what she had said. The painting was ordinary. There was nothing striking about it and it bore no comparison with some of the pictures hanging in the living room and bedroom, some of which were worth 100 yen. It was a watercolor, depicting a stream flowing past the foot of a mountain, which was densely covered with trees. On the other side of the stream was a small path which passed over an overhanging rock, parts of which were tall, parts uneven, with rocks of different sizes, and where creeping plants and wild flowers of different colors grew in a line along the rock. Further down, on a large rock almost touching the water, sat two figures. The scene was depicted from a distance, and it was not clear whether there was a man and a woman or whether they were both men. But one of them was undoubtedly a man. The words "By the Stream" appeared at the top of the painting, the artist intending this to be the title of the picture. In the bottom corner, in small letters, was the word, "Mitake," with the date below it, indicating that it had been painted six years ago.

The painting, then, was ordinary, with nothing very remarkable about it. The artist's talent was modest, and while it was quite pleasant, it was not going to provoke cries of admiration from the viewer. Someone who appreciated the beauty of nature would have expressed some interest and appreciation, but that is not a part of Pari's character. It is a pity, because it means that she and I are quite the opposite of one another.

However, it is perfectly reasonable that neither Pari, nor anyone else should show any interest in the picture, for as Pari had said, it was a very ordinary picture. But I, and I alone, think quite the reverse, for I know, all too well, the life that lies behind that painting, a life which has stamped its mark indelibly upon my heart. To other people, behind the painting there is only a sheet of cardboard, and after that, the wall. How else then, could they see it, other than as just an ordinary painting?

When I am alone, I stare at that painting and I see the water trickle lazily by and then gather speed as its course descends. I can see even the pale autumn sunlight. And the two people sitting on the overhanging rock, whom the artist has daubed in almost carelessly, I can see quite clearly. And even the long curl-ing eyelashes of one of them, and the three, bright red triangles drawn over the thin lips, giving their very thinness a wonderful charm. I know all too well that the picture was painted with the artist's life and not in some slap-dash manner. I see every move-ment in that tranquil scene; and it seems so ordinary, every scene, every part, from the beginning to the final act on which the curtain fell so tragically, only recently.

—— ONE ——

When Chao Khun Atthikanbodi took his wife, Mom Ratcha-wong Kirati to Japan for their honeymoon, I was a student at Rikkyo University, and at the time, just twenty-two years old. I had known Chao Khun in Thailand, because he and my father were friends, and he had always been kindly disposed towards me. I had also met Khunying Atthikanbodi, and got to know her as well as Chao Khun. About a year after I had gone to study in Japan,

I was saddened to hear that Khunying Atthikanbodi had died of influenza. After that, I had no further news of Chao Khun until I heard from him two years later. Chao Khun Atthi-kanbodi wrote saying that he was coming out to Japan with his new wife, Mom Ratchawong Kirati, and asking me to fix up accommodation for him and make other necessary arrangements. He was intending to stay in Tokyo for two months.

When I say he was taking his wife to Japan on their honey-moon, these are my own words; in his letter, he said he needed a change of scenery and wanted to take a long trip to relax and enjoy himself for a while. The main reason for wanting to come to Japan was to give his new wife a treat she would enjoy. Refer-ring to Mom Ratchawong Kirati, he had written, "I both love her and feel compassion for her. She is not very familiar with the outside world, despite her age. I want to give Kirati some ex-perience of the outside world, not just in Thailand, and I want to make her happy and feel that marrying someone of my age at least is not completely meaningless. I think, Nopphon, that you will like Kirati, just as you did my poor deceased wife. But for people who don't know her, Kirati is rather on the quiet side. But she's kind-hearted. There's no need for you to worry, though. I think Kirati will like you very much. I've told her that, too."

I had never met Mom Ratchawong Kirati before, and the little that Chao Khun Atthikanbodi had said about her in his letter, did not tell me very much. I guessed that she was probably about forty, or possibly a little younger. She was probably rather aloof, or at least somewhat reserved, in keeping with her aristocratic background, and certainly would not like lively, noisy young-sters, which, anyway, was not my nature. She was probably a rather serious person, with little enthusiasm for enjoying herself in the same way as most other people, and probably rather rigid in her ways, too, all of which made me cautious in my commu-nications with Chao Khun.

Chao Khun had said in his letter that he had no desire to stay in a hotel, no matter how luxurious it was, even if it was the Imperial Hotel. He was tired of having to mingle with strangers when he had nothing to do, and having to get dressed up specially, whenever he left his rooms or took his meals. He wanted to rent a house where he could be completely free, and it did not worry him how much it would cost. Of the latter, I was well aware, because Chao Khun, as well as being generous and kind-hearted, was widely known to be among the richest men in the country. I arranged for him to rent a house in Aoyamachihan District, which was a suburb not far from the railway. Travel into the city was convenient in every respect. The house I had arranged was not very large, but it was one of the more attractive ones in the district. From the outside it had a Western appear-ance, but inside, the rooms were partitioned and laid out and furnished in Japanese style. It stood on a small hill, surrounded by a wall made of large rocks about two-and-a-half feet high. Beyond the rocks was an embankment about three feet high covered in lush, green grass, with small shrubs evenly spaced along the top. Part of the inside of the grounds appeared to be covered with a dense green foliage of both large and small leaves. In front of the house stood two large trees, their branches and thick foliage covering almost the whole of the grounds, making the house appear nice and green and all the more attractive. I myself really liked it, and even though the owner wanted 200 yen a month for rent, I did not think it expensive for a nicely furnished house that had been well looked after.

I arranged for a nice-looking servant girl to look after the house in the Japanese manner. In choosing a nice-looking servant, I did not mean that she was to look after Chao Khun in any sense other than the normal duties. But I thought that if there was a choice between a servant with a face like an ogre and one with a clear, unblemished appearance, then the latter was preferable, since living close to beauty, whether in a human being or in a thing, helps to cheer us up. I was well aware that Chao Khun Atthikanbodi was in a position to be choosy. I had to pay the servant more than the normal rate; the extra expense was not for her looks, but because I had to find a Japanese girl who could speak adequate English. Otherwise, both Chao Khun and his wife would have found it troublesome.

The first day I met Chao Khun Atthikanbodi and his en-tourage at Tokyo Station was also the first great shock I was to experience in my acquaintanceship with his wife. When I first caught sight of the two women accompanying Chao Khun, I guessed that the one who was about thirty-eight, neatly-dressed, and a little stuffy and nervous, was probably Mom Ratchawong Kirati. My assumption was based on the letter Chao Khun had sent me. Her companion, on the other hand, looked young and radiant, and was elegantly dressed. Even at a first brief glance, her dignified manner was quite apparent to my eyes. I could not imagine who she was; Chao Khun's eldest daughter, who had married several years earlier, I had already met in Bangkok. My speculations, however, lasted less than a minute, because after I had exchanged a few words of greeting with Chao Khun, he turned to the young woman, who at that moment was standing beside him, and said, "This is my wife, Khunying Kirati." His introduction almost made me start at my silly mistake and I nearly forgot my manners and stared straight at her in order to dispel my doubt about what it was in her face that gave it away that she was Mom Ratchawong Kirati, Chao Khun Atthikan-bodi's new wife. She received my greetings with a graceful and gentle smile. The other woman meanwhile respectfully retired a couple of paces behind Chao Khun. As I glanced at her once more, I suddenly remembered that in his letter, Chao Khun had said that he would bring his cook out from Bangkok, too. I had completely forgotten. Ultimately, there could be no doubt as to who was who. Yet I still could not help feeling surprised that I had been so wrong in my expectations about her age and appearance.

That day I was wearing my university student uniform and that was the first thing about me that Mom Ratchawong Kirati showed an interest in. She said it was nice and neat and that what she really liked was the color—it was navy blue—which as it happened, was the same color as she was wearing, her skirt and jacket both having a white polka dot pattern. There was nothing ostentatious about the color, yet it had an indescribably proud and dignified appearance.

As I ordered the car to slow down to enter the gates of the house, Chao Khun Atthikanbodi leaned over and patted me gently on the shoulder and congratulated me for finding such a nice house. It was true that in the neighborhoods we had driven through, there was not a house to match ours. Dressed in a kimono, the servant girl stood waiting at the steps in front of the house. She bowed in greeting when the car passed through the gates, and then bowed again two or three times, in accordance with the Japanese way of showing great respect, as Chao Khun and his wife got out of the car. He spoke a few words to her and she was able to respond in adequate English, which in turn, prompted a further expression of satisfaction on his part. Finally, when he had looked over the rooms and household furnishings, he expressed his delight and thanked me profoundly once more. I must confess, I felt very pleased to have arranged everything to his satisfaction without any omissions, for my organizing abilities prompted Chao Khun to praise me later to others as "a clever chap, more circumspect than most other young men."

There was hot water prepared for baths and not a single detail had been ignored. They were both delighted from the moment they set foot in the house, and there had been no disappoint-ments to spoil the mood. In the evening I took them for a Chinese meal at Kajoen Restaurant, which was one of the most famous and luxurious restaurants in Tokyo. Both the setting and the food that evening occasioned Chao Khun to remark more than once that he was reminded of Hoi Tian Lao Restaurant in Bangkok. When we arrived back at the house, their beds had already been prepared. I returned home that night, delighted that things had gone more successfully than I had expected.

—— TWO ——

When a person becomes intimately involved with our life, the events and feelings of that first day when we met them leave a lasting impression upon our minds. That navy blue suit with the white polka dot pattern and the white hat and shoes was the first instance that the clothes a woman was wearing had made such an impression upon me. It was an outfit which I felt was proud and dignified. Mom Ratchawong Kirati was plumpish without being large. She had a healthy radiant appearance with a soft complexion. Having seen her from close quarters on several occasions, I was even more convinced of her beauty. Her large black eyes sparkled beneath long eyebrows and her cheeks glowed with health; her tiny chin curved upwards slightly and had a lovely dimple on it. Her lips were long and slender, forming two red triangles at the top with a third beneath, making them more beautiful than anything. I have to confess I had never seen such a beautiful pair of lips above such a small chin.

I knew perfectly well that Chao Khun was a fine man and I, myself, had the utmost respect for him. But despite this, I could not help but wonder what on earth it was that had induced such beauty to become wedded to an old man of over fifty. I felt curious, like any young man who wants to know and wants to understand what is going on around him. But my curiosity was casual and had nothing to do with any personal feelings for anyone. I could see that Mom Ratchawong Kirati appeared quite happy and contented in her newly married state and this whetted my curiosity still further. I was certain she was not a widow because of her fresh and radiant appearance.

Mom Ratchawong Kirati was a quiet person, as Chao Khun had previously informed me. On the journey from Tokyo Station to the house, which took about twenty minutes, she spoke to me a couple of times. When we arrived, I realized that she was even more delighted with the house I had arranged for them than Chao Khun. There was no doubt she was excited, but she kept her feelings in check as she wandered gracefully from room to room admiring the furnishings with no trace of urgen-cy or excitement. An occasional exclamation of admiration indicated her deep pleasure. She spoke little and infrequently, yet I could see the happiness in her eyes. I realized then that she was unlike any woman I had ever met.

During dinner Mom Ratchawong Kirati inquired a little about my studies and my life in Japan. I was surprised that, unlike most visitors, she did not ask about the entertainments and exciting things Tokyo had to offer, but, instead, listened with a smile as Chao Khun and I chatted. She seemed to be older than me so I felt respect for her; yet her youth and good looks still aroused my curiosity.

Chao Khun's trip to Tokyo with his wife happened to coincide with the hot season. The university term had recently ended so I was completely free. It was an excellent opportunity for me to put my time at his disposal, as and when he required it. Chao Khun was less than delighted to find Tokyo as hot as Bangkok in April. However, that had been his decision and not my advice. But when he learned that by visiting Tokyo in the hot season he was gaining the benefit of his trip coinciding with my university vacation, which could prove very useful for him, he was satisfied.

I spent almost all of the first week with the pair of them; there were only two or three occasions when I did not have lunch or dinner with them. At the beginning of his visit Chao Khun had to go and visit various friends, both Japanese and Thai, including the ambassador. In addition, he wanted to see what was going on in the country and visit various places, as is only natural for people visiting a country for the first time. I had to act as his regular guide, because, without a guide who could speak Japan-ese, getting about would have been difficult. In that first week he went to several parties arranged in his honor by both Thai and Japanese friends. There were a considerable number of people at each party and I had the opportunity to attend on each occasion.

Thus it was, that within the space of a single week, almost all of the Thais living in Japan had the chance to meet the pair of them. I knew that many were pleased to make the acquaintance of Chao Khun Atthikanbodi; but I also knew that everyone was even more delighted by Mom Ratchawong Kirati, even though she hardly knew anyone beforehand. Later, she told me that it would take her very little time to count up all the people she knew in Bangkok. It was not that Chao Khun was inferior to his wife; as I've already said, he was a fine person. But Mom Rat-chawong Kirati was a woman of exceptional charm and so, people reacted to them with different degrees of appreciation. The men were delighted to see such a good-looking Thai woman as Mom Ratchawong Kirati coming out from Thailand to visit Tokyo. It made them feel proud to see the Japanese gazing in admiration at the beauty of our women, which perhaps goes deeper than we realize. The Thai women present were no less curious and interested in her, but naturally, they did not make a great deal of fuss; they, and some of the men, too, came up and asked me about Mom Ratchawong Kirati's background, prior to her marriage to Chao Khun Atthikanbodi. At that time I was still unable to give any answer. The one thing which puzzled all of them, was what it was that had persuaded her to decide to marry her husband. People guessed that she could be no more than twenty-eight, and they could not get over it, that such a beautiful and charming woman of this age, should marry a gentleman of fifty, even if he was a fine man with the dignity and bearing of his years. I myself, however, felt especially proud at the honor of being almost Mom Ratchawong Kirati's bodyguard. It seemed to me that she must have been aware how much everyone liked her. It was true she was often quiet, but everyone could see the happiness that filled her pale pink face.

As a result of spending almost all day long with them, nearly every day, a feeling of closeness between myself and Mom Ratchawong Kirati developed rather quickly. I become fond of people quickly and everyone would agree that Mom Ratchawong Kirati was certainly someone people would be fond of. Whenever I had the chance to be near her, she would often show touches of kindness towards me, for example, serving me when we were eating, as if I were a child. On one occasion she noticed the stitching was coming loose on my tie, so she told me to take it off and then stitched it herself; another time, she noticed some mud on the cuff of my jacket, so she took it away and brushed it for me. Normally I took little interest in such matters, nor in such little niceties.

However, as I had been abroad for three years with no family to pamper me, preoccupied with my studies and leading a frugal and barren existence, it had been so long since I had encountered such kindness; and meeting it at a time when I was lonely, I found it made an even greater impression upon me. This, I myself felt was strange. I could not explain why I felt so happy sitting there close to Mom Ratchawong Kirati, waiting quietly while she stitched my tie and answering her occasional questions.

—— THREE ——

Two weeks passed and the friendship between the two of us blossomed. I saw a completely different Mom Ratchawong Kirati. She was not particularly quiet and serious, and latterly with me, she appeared to be a rather good conversationalist and someone who wanted to enjoy herself. In her own way, she could converse on both serious and light topics. When she spoke in earnest, I had the impression that she was much better read than me. It surprised me that Chao Khun Atthikanbodi should think that his wife knew little about life and the outside world. When she was enjoying herself, chatting alone with me, she would laugh loudly, her laugh full of vitality and bright, childlike innocence which echoed in one's mind long after-wards. At such moments I felt that Mom Ratchawong Kirati was a very close friend. I felt a tremendous loyalty towards her.

However, two weeks had passed and I was still unable to provide an answer to those who came asking me about Mom Ratchawong Kirati's life before her marriage, and why it was that she had married Chao Khun. It remained a mystery to me. No one would have thought she had married for love. It is not unusual to find such beauty wedded to a fifty-year-old, it is true, but for such a beauty and a fifty-year-old to love each other is unusual, for love and marriage are two entirely different matters. The majority tended towards the opinion that the power of the god, money, had played some considerable part in this instance, just as in other cases, where a woman ultimately enters into marriage, having been unable to resist the pressure. But no one dared to express such an opinion about Mom Ratchawong Kirati's marriage with any certainty, because as far as anyone knew, she was very happy with her husband.

To my mind, Mom Ratchawong Kirati was enjoying her stay in Tokyo very much. Whenever there was a chance to go out, no matter where it was, I noticed that she would take a close interest in everything around her and that her eyes would sparkle with happiness. Such curiosity, however, was unusual for someone of her age and made her appear serious. As a result, it was difficult for those who had no chance to get to know her, to feel close to her.

A new understanding developed between us while we were out walking alone together one evening during the third week. That evening Chao Khun had gone out to play golf and his wife had gone shopping at the Ginza. After she had returned and rested, she invited me out for a walk. The road we walked along was not far from the back of the house. It was a quiet road, shaded by trees on either side and hilly in parts. The fields below were lush green from the different kinds of vegetables growing there. It was quiet and peaceful with only the occasional lorry passing us. Mom Ratchawong Kirati had been out for a walk near the grounds of the house a few times and she had expressed the intention of one day walking some way down this road to have a look at the surrounding scenery. This was the first time she had put that plan into action.

We walked for a long time that day and by that time we knew each other well enough for neither of us to waste time in silence, as we had when we first met. When we were alone together we had plenty of things to talk about; when one subject was exhaust-ed there was another to take its place. Some things we talked about at great length, others only a little.

Two boys of about twelve or thirteen rode past on small bicycles, staring at us and grinning cheerfully. Mom Ratchawong Kirati smiled at them.

"I feel so happy today," she said, breathing in deeply the air around her, a soft smile still on her face.

"Why's that?" I asked. "I was afraid you might be bored because there's nothing to see."

"What do you mean, 'there's nothing to see'?" she said, pointing to the fields with their pale green lettuces stretching out before us just off to the right of our path. "Haven't you noticed the white of the leaves in the pale sunlight? What a lovely sight they are. Like velvet. And the young, chocolate-colored auber-gines. Don't they make you feel as if they're young friends of your own age? And beyond them, don't the tall lettuce plants, with their tapering leaves blowing in the gentle breeze, help to lift your spirits?"

"You sound like a poet," I laughed.

"Don't mock me. People say poets are old fashioned. I'm no poet, but if you mean I'm a poet simply because I have old-fashioned ideas, then I admit it." She smiled sweetly as she looked at me. "It's true, you know, Nopphon, these things really are the source of my happiness. You must have noticed those two children a moment ago, smiling cheerfully, and with chubby rosy cheeks and beautiful eyes. Ah, what else could be lovelier than that?"

"Now I know you're a philosopher." When I said this I do not think I was joking.

"I'm not going to say any more, because you're just flattering me," she said and walked on in silence.

"I was speaking the truth," I said hurriedly in my defence.

"All the more reason then why I'm not going to."

I stifled a smile and we walked on in silence for a while before she turned to me and spoke.

"I'm quite serious now. Wouldn't you agree with me, how full of wonder all of these things I mentioned are?"

"I wouldn't contradict you for one moment. I agree with everything you said. The reason I was going to ask, was out of concern, because generally woman aren't interested in such matters. But you're special."

"First of all I'm a poet, then a philosopher and now someone special. You're really awful, today, Nopphon. I'm just going to have to be firm."

"What, in expressing your opinion that I'm awful?"

"Yes, that too. But I meant that I'm not going to talk about such matters any more."

In her manner, which had something almost childlike about it, I saw the incomparable charm and beauty of Mom Ratcha-wong Kirati. I could only admire her and praise her in my heart.

As we approached the village, we came to a junction where there was a rundown coffee shop. Just as we walked past, a car drew up and two girls got out. Their faces were a deep pink color and they stood there unsteadily. Two men got out after them. They had taken their jackets off because of the heat and were carrying them. The eyes of one of them were half closed, while the other's were wide open and blazing. The two men put their arms around the girls and together they staggered towards the coffee shop, veering first to the left and then to the right before disappearing inside.

"A young man like you must enjoy such a spectacle," she remarked when we had passed the junction. I knew she did not mean it and was just being sarcastic, but I replied quite straightforwardly.

"On the contrary, I really hate it."

"Such ugly pleasures exist everywhere, Nopphon, in every country. Why can't they behave themselves a bit better? It's not even dark yet. And why do they have to act that way in the middle of the street? Couldn't they wait until they were out of sight? Or perhaps they think they're being very smart."

"I don't think the vast majority of people would think it was being smart. It's surely only a few people who behave that way. I've heard that in Thailand, since they opened up beer halls all over the capital, this kind of thing goes on late into the night. Is that so?"

"So I believe. But I've never seen it, and I've no idea what sort of scale it is on. I'd never have guessed that the kind of thing that happened a moment ago went on."

"But the truth is, it seems to be fairly standard for coffee shops everywhere."

"Nopphon, you're my Columbus. You've brought me to a new world."

"Are you sorry at being brought up against such sordidness?"

"I like art. I am as happy looking at millipedes and earth-worms as I am looking at stars in the sky. No, I'm not at all sorry, Nopphon. I'm grateful, even. But when you take away art from a scene like this, it disturbs me a little. But then again, it's good to be disturbed."

"You're an artist, too, perhaps both a painter and a writer," I declared in astonishment, genuine astonishment.

"Nopphon, please be careful with your words. Remember that in the space of less than half an hour, you've given me four different jobs already!'

"I think I'd be much cleverer, amazingly clever in fact, if I were to be near you for a year." I did not hear her protests, so sure was I that I had spoken the truth.

She gave me a penetrating look out of the corner of her eye, as if to see if there were any other meaning in those words. "You're so awful, it's almost cute," she said with a smile. "So all you want is one year, then?"

"I meant at least one year," I was quick to explain. "But if I had the choice, there would be no limit."

Mom Ratchawong Kirati laughed. But her laugh lacked something of its usual brightness. "But I'm going to be here for only eight weeks and already it's the third week."

"Time's passing so quickly," I said quietly. "I wish I were Hanuman."

"So you could stop the chariot of the sun?"

"But it's just impossible. I don't suppose you'd object," I continued earnestly, "if I were to ask Chao Khun to extend your stay for a bit?"

"I follow the orbit of the sun. It's not for me to choose, it's up to the sun," she replied in jest. "But don't forget your university term begins soon."

"I haven't forgotten. But I can always come to you for my education outside university hours."

After that, Mom Ratchawong Kirati asked me about my studies. When she spoke about real matters, her manner appeared serious and I became like a little child rather than her friend. We walked on for a while and came to a crowded area where people were selling things and an endless stream of traffic flowed back and forth. It was not suitable for a quiet, relaxing walk, so we decided to turn round and go back. In no time, we returned to the beauty and tranquility of nature.

—— FOUR ——

It was evening and the sun was going down as we made our way home. Little children were playing in the gardens of their homes. We passed one house set in magnificent grounds. Two healthy and good-looking young girls were, amid much laughter, walk-ing and running a toddler out of the garden and down a narrow path which led to the road we were walking along. The two girls reached the edge of the road just as we were going by. As soon as we had passed, Mom Ratchawong Kirati spoke. "What nice happy faces they had, the pair of them. What do you think of Japanese girls, Nopphon?"

"I have to confess that I find their demeanor most attractive."

"You don't think they're a bit too submissive for a man's taste, then?"

"No, I don't."

"In that case, you must be less than a man. I understood that most men liked audacious women, or at least those with a touch of audacity, and wanted some kind of wild streak or something distinctive in a woman's manner to prevent life from becoming boring."

"You may be right. But I think there are many ways of making life interesting. I may be in a minority in seeing gentleness in a woman as one of life's pleasures."

"You've been away from Thai girls for a long time. You're very much under the influence of Japanese girls," Mom Ratchawong Kirati laughed. "I think you're right," she added in a more serious tone, "and I admire your opinion, although I haven't the least expertise in such matters."

When she had finished, I thanked her.

"I can't help thinking of the happy expressions on the faces of those two girls a moment ago," she went on, almost wistfully. "They were like well-nourished plants, bursting forth into bud, ripe with life and the freshness and vigor of youth. Such radiance makes me shudder a little when I think of myself."

"I don't understand," I said, genuinely curious, "why the youth and freshness of those two young girls should make you shudder. You yourself are amply blessed in this direction, perhaps even more so than those two girls."

"Who taught you to say such things?"

"My feelings inspired me," I replied at once. "Nor do I believe I'm the only one who is convinced of this."

"But you don't know the reason for my anxiety. My beauty— if, as you seem to think, it actually exists—can't be compared with that of those two girls. They are, as I said, like buds opening up into flower. Theirs is the freshness of the dawn; mine, if it still exists, belongs to the early evening, and will soon disappear. Now, surely, you can see why I have reason to say I 'shudder.'"

"No, I still don't see," I replied with interest. "I don't even agree with your comparison, when you say that your beauty is like that of the setting sun. To me, yours is still that of the morn-ing, and even if you won't call it of the dawn, it still has a long time to shine."

"Ah, you really have such faith in me." Even though she would not accept what I had said, her delight with my words was apparent in her voice. "And that's why it is you don't realize your eyes are deceiving you. Don't you know, I'm no longer a young girl any more."

"I don't think anyone would say a woman under thirty isn't beautiful, especially in your case."

She stared at me with a triumphant look in her eyes. "You probably didn't realize I'm thirty-five."

I was stunned by her words and stared at her quite inconsiderately. Then I laughed. "You're pulling my leg. I know you're teasing me."

"What do you mean? How old do you think I am, then? Come on, quickly, tell me how old you reckon I am."

"I'd say there's no way you could be more than twenty-eight. In fact you're probably only about twenty-six."

"Twenty-six!" she cried, happiness sparkling in her eyes. "You're reminding me of how I felt nine years ago. I remember my feelings vividly. At the time life seemed full of hope. I had not the slightest premonition nor fear that I would have to marry a gentleman who was on the verge of old age. It is part of my nature to dislike decay. I might even say that sometimes I'm afraid of it. But that was nine years ago."

"And what's happened to you now?" I inquired, with growing curiosity.

"What's happened?" she asked, repeating my words slowly and gazing ahead with a distant look in her eyes. "My youth and beautiful dreams all came and went. Whether I should have let them go or not, wasn't a problem. I had to. Besides, as you can see, I married Chao Khun.

I nearly asked whether she meant she was not happy in her marriage, but common sense managed to prevail over curiosity. I realized it would have been impolite and perhaps a liberty to ask such a direct question.

"No matter how much I dislike decay and how much I love beauty, the fact is, nine years have gone by. I wish I were what you guessed," Mom Ratchawong Kirati continued, "but we can't deny the truth."

"And what is the truth?"

"The truth is, I'm not the young woman of twenty-six that you thought I was." She smiled calmly. "I wasn't fibbing or pull-ing your leg when I said I was thirty-five. I've passed what people call the "halfway mark." So I don't think I have any right to call myself a young lady."

"Shouldn't I believe my eyes rather than your words?" I said quite seriously.

"You really are the limit today, Nopphon," she said glancing at me with a lovely smile.

"In all honesty, I beg your pardon for being the limit. Hun-dreds and hundreds of people would refuse to believe you if you were to tell them you were thirty-five. Your youth and radiance is apparent even to someone with one eye closed.

"As long, of course, as the remaining eye isn't blind," she added mischievously.

"I really mean it."

"All right, Nopphon. But just so that you won't go around guessing people's ages wrongly, I'll tell you something. Women who know how to look after themselves and always take care of their health, can always look five years younger than they really are."

"But you must have been blessed by Indra or bathed in sacred fire, like Phranang Acha, to have been able to preserve your youth so amazingly well. I've never met a woman about whom I've ever been so wrong. Tell me, what's the special secret?"

"That's enough, Nopphon, quite enough," she said, waving her hand to prevent me from saying anything further. I'm not going to talk to you about it any more. You're just trying to flatter me, you know, Nopphon, all the time, and that kind of behavior spoils you."

She looked serious and walked on in silence. If she had spoken to me like that during the first few days, with such an expression on her face, I would have felt very alarmed. But since we were close enough for me to understand what she meant when she spoke like this, I merely smiled.

We arrived home at dusk. Chao Khun had not yet returned, so I stayed to keep Mom Ratchawong Kirati company for a while. When she had bathed and changed her clothes, she invited me to take a bath before dinner. She would not countenance me looking grubby or less than spotlessly clean, so my protests met with no success. But why it was that I felt strangely pleased by her concern for my welfare, I could not say.

The pleasure I had experienced talking to Mom Ratchawong Kirati that evening lingered in my mind as I walked home. Her age was something I had only just learned and it had come as a complete surprise, although I believed she was speaking the truth. If I had realized from the outset that she was thirty-five, which meant that she was thirteen years older than me, I would surely have felt that she was much my elder, and I wouldn't have been able to become close to her in the way I had. But when we ended up becoming close friends her age was no more than a shadow of the truth. I felt that Mom Ratchawong Kirati was only three or four years older than me. When she told me her real age, it did not create a barrier or make the close friend-ship that I felt for her in the slightest bit more distant. Even so, some things she had said, I had been unable to understand and, in particular, what she had said about marrying Chao Khun. Something she had said in passing had greatly aroused my curiosity. As I interpreted it, she had not married of her own free will. But I could not be certain whether my interpretation was correct. The more I thought about her marriage, the more puzzling it seemed.

Eventually, after I had got home and gone to bed, I asked myself why it was that I kept thinking about Mom Ratchawong Kirati's private affairs. What business was it of mine to have to go sorting out such problems? True, I might well regard myself as one of her friends; but why was I worrying about her personal affairs when she herself gave no indication of any concern, nor had even called upon me for any help whatsoever. Having asked myself such questions I was unable to find any answers, so I tried to banish such futile thoughts—something I felt would require considerable effort on my part.

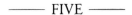

——— FIVE ———

Relations between myself and Chao Khun and Mom Ratcha-wong Kirati continued as usual. One evening three or four days later, Chao Khun received an invitation to a party. Mom Ratcha-wong Kirati said she was not feeling very well and so did not relish the thought of mingling among crowds of people, prefer-ring instead to stay at home. Chao Khun therefore asked me to stay and keep her company.

That night was the night of the waxing moon. After dinner we both had the same thought in mind—that it would be utterly foolish at such a time not to go out and enjoy the moonlight for a while. I suggested that we ought to take out a rowing boat in the public park which was only about ten minutes" walk from where we lived. Mom Ratchawong Kirati agreed.

It was still dusk when we got there. There were crowds of local people out strolling in the park. Some just sat there on benches watching others rowing on the large boating pool. We walked round the lake two or three times until we felt tired and then decided to take a boat out. There were already about four or five boats on the water, which was about the right number. That way the pool was not too noisy and crowded. I took the oars and Mom Ratchawong Kirati sat back. As we lost ourselves in conversation, I let the boat drift along on its own.

The moon was shining brightly. It was a wonderful sight, whether we watched its reflection on the surface of the water or whether we cast our eyes around the many different kinds of plants lit up in the park. Mom Ratchawong Kirati was enjoying herself and at times such as this, she talked endlessly of the beauty of nature. I agreed with everything she said, but it was not something I really took great pleasure in. In my lifetime I had experienced the beauty of the night of the waxing moon hun-dreds of times, but my eyes had never before caught sight of any living creature in the light of the moon that looked as beautiful as the woman sitting before me at that moment.

To add a little to the pleasure of the outing to the park that evening, Mom Ratchawong Kirati was wearing a silk kimono with a bold red pattern set against a white background, like a large bunch of chrysanthemums I had seen at Takarazuka Park the previous autumn. The moon was fully visible between the clouds. It shone down on the chrysanthemums all over her body making them appear alive. When she turned her face upwards, a gentle breeze blew through her hair so that it danced in the moonlight. The sparkle in her eyes was like a ray of light calling all of my attention to that one spot. She sat with her feet stretched out towards me, her pale, slender ankles tapering into firm, well-fleshed feet. She leaned back a little and abandoned herself happily to the beauties of nature.

"Don't you feel really happy, Nopphon, on a lovely night like this?" she asked softly, her eyes shining as she gazed straight at me. I was quite taken aback as I marveled at her beautiful face.

"I'm indescribably happy," I replied with enthusiasm. "More so than I can say in words."

"Doesn't it make you miss home a little?"

"I left home three years ago. I've missed it from time to time, but after a while the feeling diminishes."

"And you don't miss it at all?"

"No. At least, not at times like this."

"You're just the opposite of me. When it's quiet and my mind's filled with the beauty of nature, like now, I can't help thinking of the things I love most. I think of my father, my mother and my younger sisters at home, where it was so happy and peaceful. I think of life ten years ago when we were all living at home together, and I think of my own life then, a life that was full of hope and happiness. You're very hardhearted, you know, Nopphon, not to miss it at all at times like these."

I wanted to answer, and almost did, that in her presence, in the presence of such riveting beauty, I never thought of anything else and would have found it difficult to be able to. I dared not say this out loud, because I myself was still not clear why I had such thoughts. "I'm not hardhearted at all, but I have to take my studies seriously. Besides, if I may speak quite frankly, at the moment I'm enjoying myself being of service to you." What it was that made me reveal something of my true feelings, I do not know.

"What a man of fine words you've become!" I looked the other way. "How many more years do you have to study?" she continued.

"About five years. Because once I've finished my studies I in-tend to find a job here for a while so as to get some experience."

"That's a long time. You might end up becoming Japanese. Perhaps you'll marry one of those Japanese girls you admire so much and settle down here."

"Oh, that's impossible," I was quick to counter. "It's true I do admire Japanese progress and Japanese women, too, but that wouldn't make me become Japanese. I never forget, even for one moment, that I'm Thai and that I'm part of a Thai nation which still lags far behind other countries. The reason I've come out here to study is to seek progress for Thailand. Ultimately my goal lies in Thailand. And marriage, too."

The fact that I mentioned marriage was because Mom Ratchawong Kirati's remarks had reminded me of the girl who was my fiancée. Yes. She was merely my fiancée, whom my father had picked out for me to guarantee that I would return and marry her, or at least as a warning to me not to get involved with women over here. Since she was only my fiancée, and not a girl I loved, when I came to think of her, it was not actually of her herself, but rather of what married life would mean to me in the future.

"Your aims are very praiseworthy," she said with sincere admiration. "There are two major things that merit your attention in Thailand and they are work and marriage. What plans have you made?"

"I intend to specialize in banking because, as far as I know, there are still very few people in Thailand who are interested in this subject. So that's where my future profession probably lies. As far as marriage is concerned, I have absolutely no plans. I think it's too serious a matter to get involved in at the moment."

I felt slightly uneasy at not having told Mom Ratchawong Kirati quite clearly, that the reason I had no plans in this area was because the plans had already been made. Unless something unforeseen occurred, I would have to marry my fiancée, whom I scarcely knew, and for whom, as yet, I felt neither love nor understanding. I do not know why I did not tell Mom Ratcha-wong Kirati. Was I trying to keep it from her? I am not really sure. However, I did not lie to her or tell her something that was untrue. Perhaps I was not trying to hide anything from her because I had not been asked whether I had a fiancée waiting for me in Thailand. But supposing she had asked, how would I have answered? My heart was pounding.

"You've got a wise head on such young shoulders," Mom Ratchawong Kirati said when I finished speaking.

Our rowing boat, meanwhile, was drifting gently in the mid-dle of the pool. I picked up the oars and propelled it forwards. I was in a state of some agitation and wanted some movement which might prompt a change in the topic of conversation. Our boat was following another in which there were two girls. They were singing softly in harmony, rowing slowly and gazing up happily at the moonlight.

"They're singing nicely," Mom Ratchawong Kirati remarked quietly. "They seem quite carried away by the song. It must be a really nice one. Can you translate the words for me?"

"It's a song of consolation, not a love song," I told her when the two girls had ended their song, "telling you to be content with your station in life. In the song, it says that if we are not *sakura* flowers, we shouldn't despise being another kind of flower; all we should ask is that we might be the most beautiful of our kind. There is only one Mount Fuji, but all other moun-tains are not worthless. Even if we are not samurai, let us be the followers of samurai. We can't all be captains, because without sailors, the boat won't sail. Even if we can't be the road, let us be the pavement. There is a place in the world and work for every one of us. However great or small that work may be, every one of us, for sure, has something to do. If you can't be the sun, then be a star. Even though you weren't born a boy, don't feel slighted at being a girl. Whatever you are, then be it, no matter what it is. The important thing is we should be it to the best of our ability, regardless of what it is."

"It's a song with a very valuable message," Mom Ratchawong Kirati murmured when I had finished. "And you translated it very nicely. I'd like to hear it again. The pair of them seemed to be enjoying it so much when they were singing it."

"I see that you seem to be enjoying everything here in Tokyo," I continued after we had passed their boat. "Can you tell me why it is you're so happy?"

"Anything beautiful makes me happy. But then again, I tend to see beauty in almost everything. Just take the surface of the water with its small ripples around the edge. To me that's interesting. I love beauty because it arouses beautiful feelings."

"In that case, you'd really enjoy it if you went to stay some-where like Nikko, where the natural scenery is beautiful."

"You're right, I really would. I'd like to go to Nikko to see the waterfalls and the moonlight shining on the mountain lakes. I'd like to go to a seaside district, too, and watch the boys and girls swimming and walking together along the beach, laughing and giggling as they go. I heard Chao Khun mention that he would take me to these places soon. There's no doubt I really would enjoy it." She clasped her hands together and rested her chin upon them, a smile crossing her face as her eyes darted back and forth. "I'd like to go to Europe, too," she murmured dreamily. "I'd like to see strange new kinds of beauty. I'd like to visit England and France in winter. I'd cross over to Switzerland and then go on to Norway to see the midnight sun. And I'd end my trip in Italy, spending most of my time in Rome and Florence, where I could admire the paintings of Raphael, Leonardo, and Michaelangelo, the three great masters."

"You must be an artist, then?"

"I love art. I do a bit of drawing."

"Oh, I didn't know," I exclaimed with a mixture of surprise and delight. "It's incredible. You think everything's beautiful and you look at everything so carefully. You never told me."

"That's because I was afraid it might not be to your taste. Besides, my level of ability is nothing to boast about."

"How long have you been drawing?"

"For several years now. At least five or six. It was since I first began to feel lonely."

"If you were to go to Italy and see some good examples and get some proper instruction, maybe you'd become very famous, like those three."

"There you go again," she scolded me and frowned. "Don't try to put me on a pedestal, Nopphon, so I will at least still be able to talk to you. I draw because I really love art. In addition, I have my own personal reason, and that is, that by devoting my interest to something, it helps to ease my loneliness a great deal. It calms my mind. Have you ever thought that mental activity is like physical activity? There's a constant flow of movement, except for when we're asleep. It's part of our nature that when-ever we do something, we always have to think about it. We never stop. If we tried to be completely still, it would be like torture. You can try it now. Keep your hands still and sit perfect-ly still without moving any part of your body and without thinking of anything at all. You'll find it very uncomfortable. When you move, your movements are either beneficial to you, or not beneficial, or harmful. It's the same with our thoughts. If we don't think in a beneficial way, then we are thinking in a way which is not beneficial or which is harmful. Since our minds are perpetually active, I think that if we can find a distraction which is useful and which continually absorbs our thoughts, then life won't be worthless, and we ourselves will be able to enjoy our lives to a greater or lesser extent, regardless of our position. It's no good just letting our thoughts wander; that way we tend to end up feeling bored with life. Women in my position need a lot of things to help them in this area. If I had nothing useful to think about, I would think about useless or harmful things for sure. It's only natural. And I can say, that since I developed a love for art, art has become my good friend too. I've been going on too long. You must be bored."

"It's been most enjoyable listening to you," I said quite sincere-ly. "I'd like to—but why is it that when I offer sincere compli-ments it frightens you? Or is it my sincerity which frightens you?"

"You've answered all your questions. Is there anything else you want me to answer?"

"You're just too clever for me. At everything. I can't keep up."

"No, I think you're following your own path. You don't need to keep up with anyone. You should feel proud of yourself." She paused for a moment and pulled the sleeves of her kimono in close to her body. "It's not so humid today," she added. "There's been a breeze all day long. My feet are feeling a little chilly."

I removed the scarf from my neck and covered her pure white feet with it.

"Oh, good gracious!" she exclaimed, and then laughed softly. "Why have you covered my feet with your scarf? The two don't go together."

"Didn't you know, your feet are more beautiful than my neck? So they should receive more care."

Mom Ratchawong Kirati gave a deep sigh. It was her way of letting me know she had no wish to argue further with my com-pliments.

We were the last to leave our boats that evening. Both of us were astonished when we looked all round the pool and saw no other boat out on the water except our own. We were both surprised and amused that we had been enjoying ourselves so much that we had not realized that the others had returned to the bank. When I looked at the watch I carried with me I realized that we had spent two whole hours in the boat.

"How could that be possible?" she asked in amazement.

"I was enjoying myself with you," was my response.

"I thought it was only half an hour at the most."

"I'd have said only five minutes."

That evening Chao Khun returned home half an hour after us. Mom Ratchawong Kirati and I had each come to the conclusion that there was no need to inform Chao Khun of the details of our evening excursion, and since we were both in agreement, we did not offer each other any explanation.

That night I found it difficult to get to sleep. I wondered how I was ever going to be able to when my heart was full of Mom Ratchawong Kirati. Several questions sprang up unexpectedly in my mind. Had I ever in my life encountered a woman more charming and beautiful than Mom Ratchawong Kirati? Had I ever met a woman who had shown me the kindness and friendship that Mom Ratchawong Kirati had? The answer to all these questions was negative. Firmly and decisively negative. But why was I asking myself such questions? Why was it that I had to compare Mom Ratchawong Kirati's beauty, her intelli-gence and her other good qualities with those of everyone else—or to be more precise—with those of all the women I had previously come across? Why was I asking myself these questions? I searched for an answer. But in the end, did I ever find one?

My search lost momentum and instead of a clear answer coming to my mind, my thoughts drifted on to my feelings for Mom Ratchawong Kirati. As she had climbed out of the boat she had held out a hand for me to support her. I held her hand lightly to steady her as her feet left the boat and stepped onto dry land. As I did so, a strange feeling, one I had never felt before, ran through me. It was as if a strong hand had seized my heart and was shaking it so that I felt thoroughly unsettled. For a moment this strange feeling possessed me.

"I can stand all right now. You can let go of my hand."

When Mom Ratchawong Kirati spoke, I realized I was still clasping her hand. With a start I released that small, soft hand, but the strange feeling still pounded in my heart. What power dwelt in that tiny hand and had dragged me so far out of myself? What power was in that touch, that it still clung to my heart, even though I had come away several hours ago?

When I was leaving she came out to the main gate to see me off. As I was saying my farewell, she took my scarf, which I had forgotten, and wrapped it round my neck. "It's breezy tonight," she said. "Make sure you don't leave your collar open. I'd be sorry if you were to be ill as a result of keeping me company."

"Will you be needing me tomorrow?"

"I'll have to think about it," she replied in jest.

"Fine. Tomorrow I'll come round for your answer."

"Good. You can come round for my answer every day." She smiled happily and then said good night. "*Oyasuminasai,* my dear boy."

"*Oyasuminasai,*" I replied smiling sweetly while my heart pounded and her soft melodious voice echoed in my mind.

These were the scenes and feelings which occupied my thoughts. The moon shone down through one of the windows which I had opened slightly and onto my feet. It made me think once again of those pale, slender ankles and firm, well-fleshed feet.

—— SIX ——

Things carried on as usual, or if there was anything unusual, it was not of any great significance. A new situation, which disturbed me, arose at Kamakura at the end of summer. Kamakura is a seaside locality, about an hour's journey by train from Tokyo. It is surrounded on three sides by hills which are covered in lush, green vegetation, the remaining side opening out onto the sea. It is a seaside district of both scenic beauty and historical interest. In addition it has both Buddhist and Shinto temples and a beautiful large new Buddha image of great artistic merit, called a *daibatsu* in Japan, for which Kamakura has become famous. On Saturdays and Sundays the people of Tokyo flock there in crowds to swim and relax, because Kamakura is near enough for just a day's outing; and at weekends, especially, various amusements are arranged, catering for the trippers" particular tastes.

Chao Khun had arranged to stay at Kamakura for five days, which suited Mom Ratchawong Kirati and myself. We left Tokyo on a Wednesday. When we reached Kamakura, there were not so many people there because it was the end of the sea-son. But the Kaihin Hotel, the leading hotel in Kamakura, was still full. I had already contacted them to make advance book-ings, so we were greeted on our arrival and made very welcome. Chao Khun and his wife stayed in a twin room suite which included a bathroom and sitting room, while I stayed in a single room. They were both delighted by the splendor and majesty of the Kaihin Hotel.

By coincidence, Chao Khun met some friends at the hotel, a Japanese and an American couple. As he had some friends to talk to, Chao Khun was only too happy to allow Mom Ratchawong Kirati and me to slip away occasionally on our own. Being together day and night at Kamakura brought us very close to one another. Some days our conversation would begin at the break-fast table and others, even before that. We were together nearly all the time, sometimes in a group with Chao Khun's friends, and other times when we went out together. In the daytime we sometimes went out on a boat and other times sat and watched people playing about on the beach. In the evenings I usually excused myself and went for a swim alone in the sea, because at that time, Chao Khun normally liked to take a long walk along the beach, and I thought it only right that he should have the time to enjoy himself alone with his young wife. Thus, when he invited me to accompany them, I declined the offer, even though I could see he clearly meant it, excusing myself on the grounds that I wanted to take a swim in the sea. Chao Khun readily concurred.

One day Mom Ratchawong Kirati came down to swim with me. I could see she enjoyed it very much, even though, from what she told me, I understood she was not normally very interested in going swimming. There is one embarrassing thing about taking a Thai lady swimming with Japanese people and that is, Japanese women are not very particular about covering the upper part of their bodies and they pay little attention to their rather inadequate swimming costumes. Japanese girls may have a perfectly good reason for relaxing their caution in this matter, but our women who have been to the seaside have all averted their eyes and complained. I was afraid that Mom Ratchawong Kirati might have been bothered by it, but my fears were unfounded. She merely expressed her surprise without a word of complaint.

Our last night at Kamakura was on the Sunday. A grand ball was arranged at the Kaihin Hotel, as was customary on a Sunday night. People not staying at the hotel were allowed to join the merry-making if they purchased tickets from the hotel and that Sunday night the ballroom was packed with men and women. Besides the Japanese there were five or six Thais, including the three of us, and in addition, several Europeans, Americans and Filipinos among the crowd. Chao Khun Atthikanbodi spent the evening enjoying himself like a young man. He took the floor for many of the dances, sometimes with white ladies, sometimes with Japanese, and uncorked several bottles of champagne. Mom Ratchawong Kirati danced two or three times with friends of Chao Khun and sipped champagne, too. And I danced two or three times with a Japanese girl I knew and, likewise, sipped champagne.

As it was our last night in Kamakura, Mom Ratchawong Kirati wanted to go for a walk outside. When Chao Khun learnt of her wish, he readily consented, for he was thoroughly enjoying himself with all his friends. Mom Ratchawong Kirati invited me to go and see the various amusements. There was mini-golf and skating and we wandered around the sideshows before walking down along the beach and gazing up at the stars above. Even-tually we returned to the hotel and went and sat in the garden. Away from the crowd and alone together, surrounded by nature, we were absorbed in our own thoughts and feelings. The mixture of champagne and the soft atmosphere of the dancing had made me considerably brighter than usual. The sound of rumba music echoed from the ballroom. "Chao Khun must be really enjoying the dancing," I remarked. "The rumba music is so rousing."

"Surely he's not going to dance the rumba. It looks too fast for a man of his age. But a young man like you must like it."

"I'm not really sufficiently interested in dancing to have any special preference. They're all the same to me."

"I noticed you doing a slow fox-trot. I can see you're a good dancer."

"That was because my partner was very good."

"Who was she, your partner? She looked too tall to be Japanese."

"She's the daughter of a wealthy merchant. You're right, her manner isn't very Japanese at all, because she was born in America and lived there until she was fifteen. She came to Japan only a year before me. That's why she doesn't seem very Japan-ese. When she first met me she told me she couldn't get on very well with her own countrymen so she was happy to mix with foreigners. Whether she meant it, or whether she was just flattering us, she told me that she liked Thais in particular. She said there was something unusual about Thais—something cute."

"She was judging Thais by you."

"That's not what she said, nor what I'd want."

"Nopphon, you're a sweet and lovely boy." At these words I felt my heart racing, but before I could reply, she continued. "Earlier this evening Chao Khun told me he was very pleased to see that you and I are getting on so well. He said that you were a nice boy and that he had been quite right in guessing that I would like you a lot."

"Did he mean it quite sincerely when he said he was pleased? Is it true that he doesn't object to us being close?"

"Why do you ask?" she retorted. "Is there anything in our friendship to object to? And what makes you doubt the sincerity of Chao Khun?"

I was silent for a moment. "I'm sorry. I don't know what came over me and made me ask such a silly question. I haven't the slightest reason for doubting his sincerity."

"Are you sure?" Mom Ratchawong Kirati asked.

I was silent once again, unable to give an immediate answer.

"What's the matter with you this evening? You're not so quick with your answers as usual." She patted me gently on the arm and we smiled as our eyes met. "Are you afraid Chao Khun is jealous of you?"

I was stunned. "Why should I be afraid of that?"

"You haven't answered yet whether I guessed your thoughts correctly or not."

"You're like a fortune-teller."

"How awful," she laughed. "Why should you think Chao Khun is jealous of you? Aren't you fully worthy of his trust?"

"Isn't that for you and Chao Khun to answer?"

"Aren't your thoughts suitably innocent?"

"That's true. I shouldn't have any fears at all."

"That's right. And since your thoughts are suitably innocent, Chao Khun is not a jealous kind of man."

"I've known him a long time. He's a very kind man. That's why you must love him very much."

It was Mom Ratchawong Kirati's turn to be silent. "I like him, the way children would like a kind old man."

"You didn't say anything about love. I meant love between a husband and wife, between a man and a woman."

"You've seen what I am and what Chao Khun is. There is a big difference in our ages. It's like a large mountain acting as a barrier to the love between us and preventing our love from meeting."

"But love can exist between an old man and a young woman, can't it?"

"I don't believe in love between two such people. I don't believe it can really exist, unless we admit to ourselves that it does, and that may be a false admission."

"But you're happy in your marriage. Yet according to you, the love you each have for one another can never meet."

"The happiness a woman shows she has gained, or has, might lead most people to think that love can exist between an old man and a young woman. But when a woman is reasonably con-tented, she tends not to be interested in the problem of love. Whether there is love or not, as long as she is happy, what else does she want? That's the way people live. And most believe that love is the mother of happiness. But the way I see it, that's not always true. Love can bring bitterness and all kinds of hurt into our lives. But for those who do love, their hearts are engulfed in a wonderful sweetness which lasts forever. This isn't something I've experienced for myself. I'm speaking from what I believe."

"And what else do you want when you are already happy with life the way it is?"

"I didn't say I wanted anything else. Or to put it bluntly, as I guess you'd like, I didn't say that now I still long for love. I know I have no right to it. But I can't know whether love will come into my life or not, nor guarantee that it won't, even though I'm not looking for it. It's true that I may be happy. So please believe me, happiness without love can exist."

"And if love were to come along, what would you do?"

"Oh, I don't prepare answers to questions like that in advance because it may never happen in my life. Dwelling on that kind of thing only makes you unhappy. There's nothing sillier than worrying about something that doesn't exist or which is just a dream. Remember, "a bird in the hand is worth two in the bush" and happiness without love is better than making yourself unhappy worrying about love."

"And what about Chao Khun? Does he love you?"

"I can't answer for him. I know he's fond of me. Perhaps he loves me in the way an adult loves a child. But that's not love in the sense you mean, is it? I've already said, I don't believe in love between an old man and a young woman, so I don't expect him to love me deeply."

"You mean he doesn't want love, that he's not looking for love, even from his own wife?"

"That's right, that's what I mean. And I believe that's the truth."

"Why?"

"Because his love has dried up with old age. His days of loving have passed. Now he doesn't know how to love, because he has nothing to love with, to give me the love I need."

"But why does he seem so happy with you, then?"

"You've got a bad memory. I've already told you that you can be happy without love. He's in the same position as me."

"If it wasn't for love, why did he marry you?"

"He wanted happiness, just the same as others like him. Happiness is something human beings crave and will seek out right up until the last hour of their life, no matter how old they are. He married me because he believed it would bring him happiness."

"And what about you?" Why did you marry him, since it wasn't for love?"

"You want to know why I married him? Oh, that's a long story. There's not time tonight." Mom Ratchawong Kirati stood up. "We've been out a long time, Nopphon. Chao Khun will be waiting." I got up and as we started to walk back, she said, "You've asked me a lot of things tonight, Nopphon. I've answered a lot of ques-tions that I shouldn't have, but I thought you wanted to find out about these things."

"No," I replied quite openly. "I asked because I was interested in your life."

"If I'd known that was why you were asking I wouldn't have answered a lot of your questions. You shouldn't go taking an interest in my private life."

"You've got to admit we are very good friends."

"But that's no reason for you to go taking an interest in my inner feelings."

"Well, I have taken an interest, and you've answered all my questions."

"Because I was tricked."

"You can be tricked by happiness."

"And you're beginning to get on my nerves." Mom Ratcha-wong Kirati tugged my arm to make me walk faster. "A bit faster. I'm worried about Chao Khun."

—— SEVEN ——

Our stay at Kamakura had been enjoyable, especially the Sunday, the last night.

From our conversation in the garden of the Kaihin Hotel that night, you will have seen how far relations between myself and Mom Ratchawong Kirati had reached. You will probably have seen how close we were, and you might guess what would happen before long. But whatever your guess, I believe that it would be correct only in parts, because even I, myself, who shared a major part in the whole business with Mom Ratcha-wong Kirati, completely miscalculated the outcome of this strange, yet true story. It was a miscalculation which was to leave my heart shaken right up to this very day. But let me continue with the story.

By the time we returned from Kamakura, the rapport between Mom Ratchawong Kirati and myself had blossomed. We both felt as if we had been the closest of friends for years. We forgot entirely that our friendship had been born and had matured within the span of a single summer. We never guessed that autumn would arrive to see our friendship in full bloom. My initial position, which was merely as guide to Chao Khun and his wife when they went out on business or sightseeing, had rapidly changed. I had become an essential part in the day-to-day life of Mom Ratchawong Kirati, perhaps even *the* most essential. By that, I do not mean to boast, merely to tell the truth.

As far as I myself was concerned, I was increasingly aware that my own happiness had changed in a way that I could not understand. In the beginning I had been content merely to be of some use to Chao Khun on the grounds that I knew him from before. Subsequently that satisfaction became a need for me, a need to have as much opportunity as possible to be close to his wife. Latterly, I have to confess, the reason I gave up so much of my time to be with him and his wife, was not out of considera-tion for him, but rather out of consideration for myself. But it is certain that Chao Khun did not know this.

After returning from Kamakura, my need had reached the point where I asked myself how I would face up to it when the time came for Mom Ratchawong Kirati to leave Japan and return to Thailand. How could I face an existence without Mom Rat-chawong Kirati? I was already certain that I could not bear to see her leaving from Tokyo Station, because the train would carry her away so quickly, her tiny hand waving farewell to me, as she disappeared from sight. I had already worked it out that I would have to be with her up until the last minute. I would leave Tokyo with her when she went to catch the boat at Kobe. I would have at least an extra ten hours to be near her, and I would have a last chance to wave a lingering farewell to her at the quayside. The large ocean-going vessel would slowly and gradual-ly carry her into the distance, with none of the rapid, powerful movements of a train, which would have seemed like having her cruelly snatched from me. And I believed Mom Ratchawong Kirati would also wish our farewells to linger as long as possible.

By now, the Mom Ratchawong Kirati I had first met at Tokyo Station, who, despite her sweetness and gentleness, was rather serious and proper, had disappeared completely from my mind. It was only by conscious effort that I could recall those first images of her. The most frequent image of Mom Ratchawong Kirati which passed through my mind, was of a young woman who behaved just like a close friend. She was a friend who was both very intelligent and kind towards me. She was the nicest, sweetest woman I had ever known; someone who had brought so much joy to my empty life that it seemed almost impossible to think that she would have to leave me soon and I would have to remain in Japan for many more years without her.

By now I had been let into almost all of Mom Ratchawong Kirati's secrets and if there was anything further that I wished to know, I could find out quite easily. There was nothing I could not ask her and nothing she would not tell me. This situation continued until the day when we went alone together to Mitake. Several days prior to that, I had begun to feel that my mind was frequently slipping away from my body and into another world. It was a new world, which I saw for the first time in my life, a world glowing with beauty and happiness. The strangeness of this world seized my mind and filled it with such joy that I almost completely forgot my past. At first, I tried to prevent my thoughts from straying into this unfamiliar world. I was afraid I might find something frightening hidden there. But then I gave up trying, telling myself that there was nothing I could do to stop myself. I was incapable of with-standing the allure and excitement of this new world. I had to give my heart full rein. Finally, the day came, when I stepped into that world myself, the day when my real life touched that world: I reached the sum-mit of Everest in my relationship with Mom Ratchawong Kirati. I do not know how I managed it. I do not even know whether I meant to or not. I do not think I did. This moment of passion and intensity occurred at Mitake, in the cool gentle breeze of autumn, amid the lovely surroundings of nature. You probably recall the name Mitake. You probably remember the picture I described. An ordinary looking picture with nothing very striking about it at all. But now you are about to encounter the real life behind that picture.

——— EIGHT ———

It was a Sunday. Chao Khun had been invited to a reception by the ambassador, and so on the Saturday, Mom Ratchawong Kirati had asked his permission to go and visit Mitake with me. She arranged that I should go round and meet her at seven o'clock in the morning, which was before Chao Khun was up. Together we prepared some food in a basket and one or two other things we might need. Mom Ratchawong Kirati took a lot of pleasure in getting everything ready. We left the house at half-past eight, Mom Ratchawong Kirati not forgetting to go and say goodbye to Chao Khun in his bedroom once more. She came out smiling.

"He's just waking up," she said. "He said he was going to come and help us fix up the food and hadn't realized we'd be running away from him before daybreak. I said to him, "What do you mean, 'before daybreak'? It's gone eight o'clock." But we weren't meaning to sneak off and run away from him, were we, Nop-phon?" she said, laughing.

When we reached Shinjuku Station, it was crowded with men and women and noisy children, all waiting for the train. Mom Ratchawong Kirati had never traveled any distance by train on a Sunday, so when she saw the crowds, looking as if they were going to some big public festival, she was most surprised. I explained that it was always like this at the big stations on a Sunday morn-ing, because the Japanese loved to get out to the countryside. As a result, there were dozens of places, both of natural beauty and ones created by the authorities, and both within a short distance and further afield, which people might choose to visit, depending on their taste and means. When Sundays and public holidays came round, husbands and wives, young couples and parents with children, would all go off on outings to various such places.

"I think that finding a way for people to occupy their free time in a harmless way is one of the main factors in making Japan a strong nation," I remarked eventually. "The government make it possible for the people to buy worthwhile leisure like this at a low cost and with every facility provided. Even those on a low income have the chance to find relaxation. When I first came to Japan, I didn't think about it, but now that I've been here several years, I'm very well aware of the benefits. Most Japanese know their country well; they're hardworking and their children aren't lazy or dull because they occupy themselves in their leisure time in a useful way."

When the train drew into the station, the crowds waiting there thronged into the carriages and the seats were all filled in a moment. I had no wish to let Mom Ratchawong Kirati join them in the scramble for seats.

"It's better to wait for the next one," I told her. "It won't be so crowded."

"How many hours will we have to wait? It's a nuisance."

"In Japan we don't have to wait hours for trains. Another five minutes and there'll be another one along."

Mom Ratchawong Kirati straightened her clothes and by the time she had made up her face, another one had arrived. This time we managed to get seats, but only just, and there were others who had to wait for the one after that. We sat down next to each other on a seat for two. The Japanese on the same train stared at us in curiosity, for one thing because we were foreigners, and for another, no doubt, because of the poise and beauty of Mom Ratchawong Kirati. There were lots of children running up and down the carriage, chattering away incessantly to their parents.

"I'm exhausted but happy," she said as the train moved off a moment later. "I like the way the Japanese know how to use their leisure time, the way you explained. I hope that when you return to Thailand, you will make it possible for Thais to use their free time in a way which is both useful and enjoyable. I believe you could do it, because you've been educated abroad. Most people have great faith in the ideas of those who've been educated abroad."

"So I've heard. That's the way I thought when I was still in Thailand. But when I became one of those studying abroad myself, and saw what my fellow students here were like, I felt that we were praised too much. We have a better opportunity than students in our own country, in that we see an example of progress which we don't have in Thailand. But if we don't take full advantage of this great opportunity, we won't have any special qualities to back up our claim to being better than others. Apart from that, there are more opportunities for us to come to grief than for students in Thailand. The more prosperous a country is, the more distractions it has to lead you down the path to ruin. And as you see, we live here without any supervision. We have to battle against many distractions on our own. You can see how easy it is for us to lose that struggle. It's not all of us who win. There are both winners and losers. What special quali-ties do we have, what special rights, to march out at the front as if we are more special than anyone else in Thai society?"

"What you say is very true, Nopphon. I don't know very much about those educated overseas myself. I only go by what I've heard. But since I got to know you, I've became interested about students who study abroad. In all sincerity, I judge such students by you."

"You praise me too much. To tell you the truth, I don't like people to be too nice towards us, nor to hope for too much from us, because if they're disappointed, they might blame us for deceiving them, even though, in truth, you've already seen that I've never thought of deceiving you."

Mom Ratchawong Kirati laughed with delight and we chatted on about these problems for a while, and then on to other things and admiring the scenery on either side of the road. Our journey took about an hour and a half. It was a journey which Mom Ratchawong Kirati said was not in the least bit boring.

About half of the passengers, ourselves included, alighted at Mitake Station. As we left the station and approached the main road, we could see how beautiful the scenery was. There was a broad stream and rocky slope and our eyes were filled with the green of dense vegetation. Mom Ratchawong Kirati seemed very happy. We walked around admiring the scenery and looking at the shops for a while and then stopped at one for a rest and a drink. I had told Mom Ratchawong Kirati that it was rather crowded there and that I would take her on further by bus, which would run parallel to the stream until it reached the slopes of Mount Mitake. There we would be alone together in the peaceful surroundings of nature; that was our destination that day, in our search for happiness.

When we had rested and seen enough there, we continued on our way by bus for another forty minutes or so. The bus ran parallel to the stream, where the water was so sparkling and clean that it was possible to see the jagged stones lying beneath the surface of the water. On the other side of the road the slopes were bright green with the foliage of many different kinds of trees, both large and small. The bus drove past ordinary people who had decided to walk. All along the route there were old people, young men and women and children, all looking as if they were really enjoying their walk.

We reached our destination a little after mid-day. Few people had decided to come this far since all along the route there were resting places with magnificent views, which those who were not going so far would stop off at. So when we got off the bus and walked down the evenly sloping path, there were only two people who followed us, a middle-aged man and his son of about twelve. Whether he had come along to keep his son company, or whether he had brought his son along to keep him company, we did not know.

The path descended until eventually it reached the stream. We came to a waterfall which was the source of the wide stream we had passed earlier. The water poured down onto the stones and then flowed, with a strong current in places, in a trickle in others, down into the stream, which gradually became broader. The path that we walked along was surrounded by steep slopes that were bright green with various kinds of vegetation. We went down and stood on the stones, so that the water flowed right past our shoes. Both Mom Ratchawong Kirati and I were like a pair of children as we played about, jumping from stone to stone. We could enjoy ourselves in complete freedom, because there, you could almost say, we had come to a new world, inhabited only by the stream, the rocks, and the woods. The sun warmed us without being too hot. The middle-aged man and his son had disappeared from sight. Occasionally a couple would pass through our world, but they never stopped for long. Thus, we were like Adam and Eve in that small world. I picked a purple flower and asked to pin it to her hair, and she picked a different kind, a red flower, and stuck it in the buttonhole of my jacket. She told me she was really glad that I had brought her to a place filled with the fragrant scent of tranquility and the beauty of nature. I told her I was very pleased to have had a part in bring-ing her happiness or bringing her to happiness.

I can still vividly recall my feelings that day. That I was happy and in high spirits goes without saying. But even so, certain feelings disturbed my happiness, causing my heart to beat faster in apprehension that something overwhelming would happen. Hour after hour they churned up and down in my heart. It seemed I tried to hold them back, but I felt it was almost beyond me. All I could do was wait. I was both exhausted and happy.

—— NINE ——

After lunch and a rest, we set off along the main path which led up the hillside. There were no houses along the way. Far ahead, high up on the top of a hill, there were four or five huts, indicat-ing that people lived there. They raised crops for their living, and that small territory on the top of the hill was their world. We arrived at our destination at the summit of the hill without en-countering a single tourist on the way. We sat down to rest in the shade of the spreading boughs of a cedar tree.

I shall not describe in detail how we passed our time there. I shall describe part of a conversation which revealed very clearly everything about Mom Ratchawong Kirati's life. Once again, I brought up the subject we had talked about in the gardens of the Kaihin Hotel.

"I'd like to know what your reason was for deciding to marry Chao Khun."

"You seem very interested in the business of marriage. Is it something you're getting yourself ready for?"

"No, no," I hastened to reply. "I certainly wasn't thinking about getting ready for my own marriage. I'm not even interested in the business of marriage in general. It's just you I'm interested in."

"And why do you have to be interested in my personal affairs which are, after all, private?"

"Didn't you say you regarded me as one of your very closest friends, of whom there seems to be only one?"

"But why do you want to know?" she asked with resignation. "My life is one of misfortune. My reasons for getting married were those of a woman who has been most unfortunate in love. There's no example there for you to note, and it may make you feel sad, or feel pity, or feel that my misfortune served me right. There's nothing very enjoyable about it. You've gotten to know me under my present circumstances which is fine and should be enough. You shouldn't know too much about my life in the past. It might spoil your happiness."

"I'm not a coward, nor faint-hearted. The more I know it has to do with your misfortune, the more I feel I need to hear it."

"Nopphon, you're always so earnest," she said, beginning to smile in an affectionate way. "I never manage to put you off."

"Your two younger sisters are already married, aren't they?" I began.

"They married seven or eight years before me. Now they're living happily with their husbands, and not old husbands, either. And not only happily, either, because they have both happiness and love, too."

"It's very sad."

"That my younger sisters are happy and love their husbands?"

"No, I'm very glad about that. I'm sorry about you."

"Do you want to tell me what you think, or do you want to hear it from my mouth?"

"I'm ready and listening."

"You already know that I married Chao Khun without loving him," Mom Ratchawong Kirati began. "What you want to know now, is why I married him even though I didn't love him. For you to fully understand, I shall have to enlighten you on another important matter first, and that is the question of why I married at the age of thirty-five. It's too old for a woman getting married for the first time. You must know that generally, girls get married between the ages of twenty and twenty-five, or at the latest, or worst, not after—or it shouldn't be after—the age of thirty. So why was it that I got married when I was nearly thirty-five? It's too old. You mustn't try to take my side by saying I still look very young. You have to admit that it really is too old, whatever the reason. You never raised this question before. Perhaps it was something you overlooked, thinking it wasn't an important problem. But I myself know very well that it is important, so important, in fact, that it might be regarded as the source of the subsequent problem—that is, why I married someone I didn't love. I'll give you answers to both of these problems, so that you'll understand me as clearly as if you were gazing at the sky on a cloudless day. I want to quench your curiosity so completely that you'll stop bothering me with questions."

Mom Ratchawong Kirati paused and stared at me as I sat in a meditative posture right at her feet, paying close attention to her words. We were sitting on a large floral-patterned blanket, big enough for us to lie down on, even though we did not. Mom Ratchawong Kirati sat leaning against the cedar tree, a cushion behind her back.

"I really would like to know why you waited so long before you got married. It was silly of me not to have asked."

"It's silly of you to be always flattering me for still looking so young," she said, half in jest, half seriously. "I have just got married, but it wasn't that I put off marriage. When I say this, you may well imagine that as a young girl, my life was full of strange and wonderful things, with its fair share of love and sorrow. So as not to let you waste your time guessing, then, for you'd be sure to guess wrong, let me tell you in advance, that in my life there was no love, no sorrow, no shedding of tears, no feelings of being transported to heaven, nor to the depths of hell, or anything exciting like that at all. My life was far removed from such things. My life consisted of ordinary events, too ordinary, perhaps, which led to disappointment and made me such an unfortunate woman."

"I don't want to interrupt, but I find it hard to believe that in a life such as yours, where there is some considerable problem, there isn't at least something strange or unusual hidden away. I can't help wondering."

"My dear boy, you should give up your studies and take up fortune-telling, because you always know more about my life than I do myself.

"When I was a girl," Mom Ratchawong Kirati continued, "I led a very narrow life. While I was growing up, I had no chance to enjoy myself the way ordinary girls do. I didn't intend to keep myself apart from other women at all, but I was in fact kept apart.

I wasn't a *chao,* but the daughter of one. My father was a real *chao nai.* Before the end of the absolute monarchy, most *chao nai*, as you know, really behaved like *chao nai.* They lived in a different world. My father tried to make me and his other children like him. At first I went to school regularly, like anyone else. Then when I reached adolescence, he kept me shut away in his world. He shielded me from contact with the outside world. I continued my education with an elderly English governess at home, or at the palace, as it was called in those days. I learned about the outside world from my English governess and from elderly English women. There didn't seem to be much difference between my elderly English governess and elderly Thai ladies. Her conversation was all to do with moral virtues and house-keeping and that kind of thing. It was fortunate that she intro-duced me to the existence of the magazines, *Vogue* and *McCalls*, which gave me advice on how to take care of and preserve my youth and beauty for a long time, so that it would be like the lasting freshness of the hydrangea.

"So I stayed at home, studying with my governess. Sometimes my father would send me to the palace to wait upon various senior princesses who were relatives of ours. As a girl, I spent several years in this manner. I lived in the world of *chao nai* for so long, I scarcely had the chance to realize just how precious youth is to the female sex, and that I should be using my youth for my own benefit. At the time, it seems I never asked myself whether it was right that we should shut away our youth from the eyes of the outside world, what good it did to our lives, and whether it was clever to keep hidden our most beautiful years. At the time I never thought about it, because we hadn't been trained to think. The path was fixed for us, and we had to walk down that narrow way in accordance with tradition."

At this point Mom Ratchawong Kirati paused for a moment and I seized the opportunity to interrupt. "But that doesn't sound like the you I know. You're clever and thoughtful and much smarter than ordinary people like me."

"Please don't say I'm cleverer than you or anyone else. If I can just manage to hold my own amongst others, that's good enough for me. It was events over the years that followed that taught me to think. And then my English governess used to find me good English books to read so as to awaken in me a love for books. And then I love art, and every kind of beauty, and so I came to be more reflective. I think I have a natural inclination in this direction, so it was only for my own satisfaction that I took care of my looks and appearances at that time. I've already told you that I had no thoughts of doing anything to capitalize on my youth."

"I sympathize with you being in such a position," I interjected.

"But art came to my aid," she went on. "I have little time to spend reflecting and and feeling lonely. I have work to do nearly all day long. I'm interested in drawing and, as you know, I spend a lot of time practicing. I get a lot of pleasure from it. Besides that, I have another kind of regular work, and that is taking care of my looks so that they will last as long as possible. I have to spend several hours a day on my regular routine."

"That's scarcely believable," I said doubtfully. "What do you have to do for several hours every day? One hour should be enough for powdering yourself, making up your face and putting lipstick on."

She smiled, her eyes sparkling with high spirits. "Actually, there's more to it than you might think. You can't understand everything about a woman. Anyway, I hope you're not sudden-ly going to criticize me for wasting several hours a day on something useless. Have some sympathy for the female sex. We're born to be decorations, to please the world, and in order to perform these duties to the best of our ability, we have to preserve our appearances. Of course, that's not the only duty of the female sex. But you wouldn't deny, I'm sure, that it is one of them."

"I certainly wouldn't disagree with you, because over and above virtue, men seek beauty in the female sex."

"What's more," said Mom Ratchawong Kirati emphatically, "a good woman is sometimes completely overlooked if she is not beautiful as well. When my youngest sister got married, although I sometimes used to dream of love, I lived on happily in hope for a further two years until my other younger sister married the man she loved. It was at that time that I first began to feel I was unlucky. At that time I was twenty-nine and my sister was twenty-six. Her marriage and the happiness it brought her pierced my feelings. Believe me, Nopphon, I'm not jealous of my sister. I love her more than I love myself. But I felt pity for my own fate. Up until now it's been difficult to tell you how I really feel, because it might have looked as if I were showing off or had some indecent thoughts in mind. Do you think you really understand me?"

"I'm your closest friend. I feel for you and understand you better than anyone."

"Do you fully believe in my moral principles?"

"I have no doubts whatsoever."

"Are you sure?"

"Absolutely, without the slightest wavering."

"Your assurance sounds as solid as a pledge. So I shall tell you my feelings, honestly and sincerely." She gazed past me, her eyes still sparkling, it was true, but with a tinge of sadness. "When I was twenty-nine, I was still beautiful and looked more radiant and youthful than my younger sisters. I was lucky to have been born with beauty but unlucky to be without love. It may have been because of that beauty that I was shielded from and prevented from making contact with the outside world more than my younger sisters. I wouldn't feel unfortunate if I'd been born plain. But when he bestowed beauty upon me, why didn't God, or whatever sacred powers there might be, make an open-ing for me? Why has my beauty been cast aside to loneliness and solitude, the beauty I have fought to cherish and preserve in a way that few women could match?"

At this point the sadness was clearly visible in her eyes. "When my younger sisters were both married, I felt more and more lonely. But when I considered my beauty and youthful appear-ance then, at the age of twenty-nine, I still had hopes of finding love and marrying a man whom I loved. Nopphon, you mustn't think my frank account of my feelings indecent. Love is a wonderful blessing. It is the ultimate in life. Like everybody else, I liked to dream of love and marriage. I longed for the oppor-tunity to talk about, and experience for myself, life in the new world, just as my two younger sisters had had. I longed to have a house of my own and to mix with the outside world. I longed for children, on whom I could lavish the love and tenderness in my heart; I longed for my lap and my arms to benefit another. And I longed for many other wonderful things which I could have attained if only I had found love.

"To reach the age of twenty-nine without finding love is bad enough. But for me it was especially unfortunate. Year after year, my dreams came to nothing. My hopes gradually faded, until, at the age of thirty-four, Chao Khun Atthikanbodi came into con-sideration. Chao Khun and my father were very good friends. As he grew older, my father ceased to think very seriously about anything. So when Chao Khun expressed a wish to marry his eldest daughter, who had been stuck in the house for a long time already, he was happy to grant Chao Khun's wish. He thought, in all sincerity, that Chao

Khun's request was the last remaining chance for me to get married. He feared that if I refused, it would be tantamount to saying no to marriage for the rest of my life. And if that were in fact to be the case, he would have been sad-dened by my fate. I knew very well that my father loved me and, of all his children, was concerned the most for me. He wanted to see me married so that I would have my fair share of happiness. He thought that for a beautiful woman like me to go through life without a husband was more than he could bear to see. However, he merely advised me and implored me to accept Chao Khun's offer; the final decision was left to me."

Her eyes met mine and she smiled a sad and candid smile. My heart melted before the sorrow in that smile and that beautiful pair of eyes.

"When I learned of Chao Khun's wish, I was stunned, and when I heard my father advising me and pleading with me to agree to marrying Chao Khun, I cried. I cried with a mixture of alarm and many other feelings. My father understood me very well. "My child," he said, consoling me, "I don't underestimate you. I feel for you very much. You're the best and most beautiful of all my children. I'm more proud of you than I can tell you. I know perfectly well that a match with someone who is getting on in years, like Chao Khun, is not suitable. I would wish that you could marry a man you loved of a fitting age and family background. But fate has dealt unjustly with you. It saddens me so much when I think what a good and beautiful girl you are. But you're nearly thirty-five, now. Marry him, my child, marry the man I suggest. Even though he's old, he's a good man."

"I hardly said a thing to my father. I remember that all I did was cry. My father comforted me. He kissed me on the forehead in pity and then left me alone. That evening, I dressed myself up immaculately and sat in front of the mirror in my bedroom. For a long while I examined my physical appearance with painstaking care. I still had the figure of a young girl and my looks were without blemish. It was awful to think that this body, which was still young and fresh with beauty, would have to be wedded to a man of fifty. Was it true that this beautiful figure could exist unloved and with no hope of love? I didn't believe it was possible. But when I remembered how old I was, I felt alarmed once more. Tears poured down my face when I realized that Chao Khun's request was a symbol of the disintegration of my hopes, a symbol that my chance of finding love and marrying a man I loved had completely gone. My time was up.

"For two or three days after, my father didn't mention the matter. He waited quietly for my answer. I chose what were, under the circumstances, my most rational moments, to think seriously about my decision. Eventually, I decided to accept Chao Khun's offer.

"Why didn't you say no? You look so young and beautiful, even now," I said in all sincerity. "You were sure to find love if you'd waited a bit longer. You really should have said no."

"You talk as if things hadn't yet happened, Nopphon," she said with a faint smile.

"The world is very cruel," I complained.

"People might be cruel. But the world is lovely, isn't it, if you just look all around you right now?" She paused and stared at me for a moment. "I'm going to tell you the reason why I decided to agree."

"I can't see any reason. I don't think it could have been a very good one."

"My dear boy, please don't be bad-tempered and please don't forget that we're talking about something that is past, that has already happened. There's nothing for us to quarrel about."

—— TEN ——

Mom Ratchawong Kirati continued with her story. "My father's pleas were one reason why I considered Chao Khun's wishes with much less bitterness. I knew that if I refused, it would disappoint and sadden him very much. But that wasn't the main reason. The main reason was because I wanted to. I had had to spend a full thirty-four years of my life in a confined world. I was thoroughly bored and lonely. Even a tiny bird leaves its nest when its wings are strong and flies around, seeing the great wide world. And I'm a human being and fully grown —to the point of being on the downward path—so why should I stay in the same place? I wanted contact with the outside world. I needed a change in my life. I needed something that was different from what I had been doing for thirty-four years. The only thing that was going to help me achieve this, was marriage. I was extremely unfortunate not to have love, but even so, would it have been clever to close my eyes and shut off my feelings to other things which might offer some measure of enjoyment? Since Chao Khun was a kind man, how was I going to be worse off? He was too old for me to marry, it's true; but who was it, then, that I was waiting for? I might have waited for somebody, but who? Where was I going to meet him? In fact, he might not even have been born yet, or he might have just died. At the time, I badly needed something real. I decided to resign myself to marrying Chao Khun because that was real. I would achieve many of the things I wanted to. I'm glad to have got to know and become familiar with many strange things in a different world. I am happy enough, even without love."

Mom Ratchawong Kirati adjusted her position and sat up straight. She gave a deep sigh and wiped her eyes with her handkerchief. "Nopphon, I feel as if I've been in a dream while I've been telling you all this. Perhaps I rambled on a bit so I'll stop now."

"I'm absolutely fascinated by your story. Perhaps it seems only an ordinary one but it certainly held my attention. Can I ask you a few more things? Don't you think that one day you might be able to love Chao Khun?"

"I seem to have already told you once that there is no way I can love him. Of course he's a really good man. But what do I want with an old man? He wants to eat his fill and go to sleep and to enjoy himself in his own way. He has too little time left for building ideals in life. He's not interested in moonlight and lakes or even sweet words. He has no thoughts nor dreams of beauty. He has no future; only a past and a present. So how can you expect love to blossom forth? Even a rose won't bloom on a concrete road."

"Happiness without love. Doesn't that seem rather barren?"

"Nopphon, don't tie me up with so many questions. I can't breathe. Give me a bit of freedom." Her eyes met mine and she smiled gently. The sadness had disappeared from her eyes and there was a bright sparkle there instead. She took out a mirror and spent a moment doing her face and hair. I looked at her closely, in wonder.

"Are you happy, today?" I asked, my voice trembling slightly. She gave a slight nod by way of reply, and in her eyes there was a hint of danger which increased my sense of wonder.

"It's getting late, Nopphon. We'd better start getting ready to go back." She began to get up. "Ooh, my legs are all numb because we've been sitting down too long. I'm hardly going to be able to walk back down."

"I'll carry you," I said. I got up and put my arm around her to support her. She declined my assistance in a quiet voice, but I took no notice. When she was on her feet, I was still holding her arm and standing close to her. "Are you very happy?" I asked.

"Looking down to the stream from up here, I feel as if we've come up a very long way. I'm still wondering how I'm going to have the energy to get back down."

I moved closer to her until our bodies were almost touching. Mom Ratchawong Kirati leaned back against the cedar tree. I knew that both our hearts were pounding fiercely.

"When we get down there I'm going to do a sketch of two figures," she said.

"I'm so happy when I'm as close to you as this."

"And when are you going to let go of me so that we can get our things together?"

"I don't want to be any further apart." I drew her body up close against mine.

"Nopphon, don't look at me like that," she said, her voice beginning to tremble. "Let go now. I'm strong enough to support myself."

My face buried itself against her soft pink cheeks. I no longer had the strength to restrain myself. I held her close to me and kissed her passionately. For a moment I was unconscious, lost in oblivion.

Mom Ratchawong Kirati released my grip and gradually pushed me away from her. I did not resist. I had rapidly been transformed into a lamb. She leaned back against the tree. She was breathing heavily as if she had walked a long way and was tired. The pink hue of her face had turned a dark color as if she had been burned by the sun's heat.

"Nopphon, you don't know what you've just done," she said, her voice still shaking.

"I know I love you."

"And is it appropriate, then, that you should express your love for me in such a way?"

"I don't know whether it's appropriate or not, but love got the better of me. It completely overpowered me and left me senseless."

Mom Ratchawong Kirati gazed at me with a sad look in her eyes. "Do you express your love at times when you're senseless? Didn't you know that there's nothing you later regret more than the things you do when you're senseless?"

"But I know for sure that I honestly love you."

"And what meaning is there in expressing love when you're senseless?"

"I love you, genuinely, with my heart and soul. What I did, will remain imprinted upon my heart."

"And do you think it will be profitable for your life if it is imprinted upon your heart?"

"In love, do we still think about capital and profit?"

"You might not and I might not. But love might think of us in such terms. Haven't you ever thought," Mom Ratchawong Kirati continued, "of the position I'm in and the position you're in?"

"I've thought of it a great deal."

"And yet you still behave the way you did towards me a moment ago. Don't you realize, you acted quite unreasonably and, as you yourself admit, thoughtlessly?

I stood crestfallen with my arms folded. "I feel absolutely terrible. I don't know what to say to redeem myself. All I know for sure is that I was overcome by love. Even though it's true that what I did was wrong, I'm subject to the laws of nature. I tried to escape them, but when I came face to face with love, I couldn't and I was forced into a corner. I beg you not to bring reason into it, nor right and wrong. I have no answer. These came after the laws of nature and we are all subject to her laws."

"Nopphon, if the two of us were to spend the rest of our lives on the top of Mount Mitake, then everything you say would be correct. But in reality, in a moment we'll go down this mountain and face other people. And before long, you'll have to go back to your studies and ambitious plans for the future. As for me, it's my duty to be loyal to Chao Khun, to follow him wherever he goes, to look after him and wait upon him like a good wife for as long as he still wants me and as long as he doesn't neglect his own obligations. You and I will soon have to part and each of us will have to mix in society, which is strict on matters of reason and right and wrong. So how is it you can want me not to mention them? Do you think society would accept the laws of nature which you offer as an excuse? Nopphon, please believe me. You must try to face up to reality. Truth is the only judge in our lives. Laws and ideals might be more attractive, but in practice, they are worthless."

I felt I was facing a woman who was too rational and intelligent for me to keep up with. She should have been a character out of history instead of Mom Ratchawong Kirati, an ordinary woman of today. "I'm very sorry if I've displeased you," I said quietly. There was nothing else I could say.

"You upset me."

"Please answer just one question. Do you believe I love you?"

"I believe you."

"Are you very cross with me for what I did?"

"I've already told you, you don't know what you did. Some day you'll find the answer yourself, and you'll feel sorry."

"Do you hate me now?"

"If you don't refer to what happened today again, I'll feel that you're still the same old Nopphon, and will be, all my life."

"And I may still love you with all my heart and soul?"

"That is your right. But as time goes by, you will happily relinquish that right of your own accord."

"I'm certain my love for you will never fade."

"At your age, people have great confidence in themselves. But we'll have to wait and see. I congratulate you on your confidence."

"Are my feelings reciprocated?"

Mom Ratchawong Kirati moved closer and stood almost touching me. She put her hands on my shoulders and said, "My dear boy, I forgive you. We'll both forget what happened today. You must go back to being the old Nopphon and be cheerful and happy from now on. Now let's hurry up and get everything ready to go back. Chao Khun will be concerned if we're very late back."

I sensed an almost regal authority in her voice and I had not the courage to suggest otherwise. Having spoken, Mom Ratchawong Kirati wasted no time in getting down to packing things up into her bag. I stood for a moment with my arms folded, watching her absorbed in packing up, until she urged me a second time, whereupon I began to help her. On the way back, she chatted quite naturally about this and that, as if the most significant event in our lives had not taken place on that mountain.

——— ELEVEN ———

When we got off the train at Shinjuku, the streets were already lit up.

"Nopphon, you're looking gloomy," Mom Ratchawong Kirati warned me as we drove back to the house. "You must be careful how you act when we get home. And don't show any sign of alarm in front of Chao Khun. We're a bit late getting back. If your behavior seems different, he might begin to think."

"Think what?" I asked, slightly disconcerted.

"I can't guess what he might think, but it's better if we don't do anything unusual to make him think."

I said I would try. When the cab pulled up in front of the house, Mom Ratchawong Kirati stepped out lightly. My heart was pounding slightly.

"Are you ready, Nopphon?" she asked me softly.

I nodded and smiled in an attempt to convince her that I was not the sort to panic. The maid informed us that Chao Khun had not yet returned from his party. I heaved a deep sigh of relief. At that point I really did cease to panic.

That night I left Mom Ratchawong Kirati at nine o'clock. I did not go straight home for there was nothing for me to return for. I would not have been able to concentrate on my books and even if I had tried to force myself to go to sleep, I would not have been able to, for my mind was ablaze with different thoughts and emotions. There was no point in going home. After leaving Mom Ratchawong Kirati's house, I took a cab back into town. Tokyo was all lit up. I got off in front of Ueno Park and wander-ed around its large and beautiful gardens. I walked along, oblivious to my surroundings and fellow strollers. It was just that there was a path there, so I followed it, engrossed in my thoughts. When I began to feel tired, I went and sat by the edge of the lake. Exhausted by the day's outing, I lay back and stretched out, trying to recall what I had done to Mom Ratchawong Kirati that afternoon on Mount Mitake. I had held her close and kissed her passionately, and I had told her how much I loved her. Had I really gone that far? Had I really dared to tell Mom Ratchawong Kirati, the wife of Chao Khun Atthikanbodi, for whom I had so much respect, that I loved her, and kissed her, too? I had indeed. It was true.

Whether I was happy or sad at what I had done, burdened or relieved, I could not say for sure. Even so, I wanted to know. One thing I was certain of, was that I loved Mom Ratchawong Kirati with all my heart, loved her, utterly and completely.

I tried asking myself whether I needed Mom Ratchawong Kirati or not. I felt that without her I would be so lonely and miss her so much. Could you call this not needing her? Yet I had no right whatsoever to claim I needed her when she already belonged to someone else. In which case, was I going to snatch her away? I had no such intentions. I was still in the middle of my studies, and in addition, Chao Khun was someone I respect-ed. Besides, I was not so bold as to presume that Mom Ratcha-wong Kirati would ruin her reputation for the sake of my love, or, perhaps, also for the sake of her love. So I could not really say whether I was happy or not at what I had done to express my love openly to Mom Ratchawong Kirati. My mind was filled with confusion. Eventually I came to the conclusion that it was not suitable to become too preoccupied with these problems in a quiet, peaceful place such as this. I left Ueno Park and took a cab. Along the streets, still teeming with crowds, we drove, past one and out into another, with no clear destination in mind. Eventually I got the cab to drop me off at a coffee shop, a reasonable one, that was not too low class.

In fact I was not very familiar with such places. On occasions I had brought other people to this one. The reason I was bold enough to go in alone that day was because I needed a change and a bit of relaxation as a relief from all the problems on my mind. As I went up the steps, a lovely young girl came out to greet me. I was surprised when she said she recognized me, even though I visited the premises so infrequently. She explained that the reason why she recognized me so readily was because I spoke her language better than any other Thais who went there. Besides, she told me, she clearly remembered my polite manners as well as my language. I thanked her.

About five minutes into my first glass of beer, I began to feel less burdened and more cheerful, as I chatted and joked with the girl in the usual way, while she sat waiting upon me, pouring my beer and lighting my cigarette. My mind had turned to happier thoughts. The sensations I had experienced when I embraced Mom Ratchawong Kirati and kissed her passionately, returned to me once more. I sipped my beer as I recalled those moments. Ah, how happy I was to think that I had won love, won the heart of such a charming and intelligent and wonderful woman as Mom Ratchawong Kirati. Such thoughts gave me great pleasure and I chatted with the girl waiting on me and pulled her leg. A little more than an hour later I left and walked home in a daze, not, this time, under the weight of countless problems, but as a result of the beer which had helped to cheer me up.

Once I got home, I did not retire immediately, and it was past one o'clock before I finally want to bed. But one problem pursued me, even after I had closed my eyes: was I correct in thinking that I had won Mom Ratchawong Kirati's love, that I had won her heart? Had Mom Ratchawong Kirati told me as much? I realized then that Mom Ratchawong Kirati had said no such thing. Eventually, however, I fell asleep, even though the problem remained partly unresolved.

―――― TWELVE ――――

The day we visited Mount Mitake was the beginning of the eighth week. According to their original plans, Chao Khun and Mom Ratchawong Kirati were to leave Tokyo and return to Thailand at some time during that week. But a couple of days later, I learned from Mom Ratchawong Kirati that Chao Khun was happy to extend their stay in Tokyo by a further two weeks. During this period there were two major items on their itinerary. Firstly, Chao Khun and Mom Ratchawong Kirati would spend two or three days at Atami in order to bathe in the hot springs and see the scenery, for which it was famous throughout Japan. And secondly, on the journey from Tokyo to Kobe, they would stop over at Osaka for two or three days to see the progress of one of Japan's major industrial cities, and also, the Takarazuka Theater, which was the biggest in Japan.

In the days that remained, I went to see Mom Ratchawong Kirati and Chao Khun just as before. I have to confess that latter-ly, when I was with Mom Ratchawong Kirati in the presence of her husband, my conscience was not as clear as it had once been, and I had to make a constant effort so as not to behave in an unnatural way. The churning feeling in my heart must have been no different from the feelings of a criminal who, having secretly committed a serious crime, then mixes with upright people.

It surprised me very much to see that there was nothing in the least unusual in Mom Ratchawong Kirati's demeanor. She remained just as warm to me as before, whether her husband was there or not. The warmth she showed towards me in the presence of Chao Khun in particular, frequently caused me alarm. However, the fact that she had behaved quite normally towards me throughout, was a relief to me, that she was still the same Mom Ratchawong Kirati as before, and that she did not hate me after I had caused such a disturbing incident on Mount Mitake. Once or twice I tried to bring it up, but her response cut me short.

One evening at Atami, Mom Ratchawong Kirati invited me out alone with her for a walk.

"There's only six days left." We were talking about having to part.

"You keep counting the days then, do you, Nopphon?"

"I count every hour, every minute, almost every breath."

"You're taking it much too seriously. I warn you, my dear, you might be ill. You must try to control yourself." Her voice was full of kindness, a voice which pierced my heart even more deeply.

"I don't want to. I don't see any reason why I should have to suppress a love which arose spontaneously and purely, a love which is innocent and tragic. I can't do that to love."

Mom Ratchawong Kirati sighed. "We can't escape reality, Nopphon."

"What reality?"

"The reality that we must part in six days time."

"It's a very cruel reality," I said bitterly.

"That's why I asked you to try to control your feelings. Please believe me, my dear."

"I'll try. But I don't think it will be any use."

"We should never have met," Mom Ratchawong Kirati said wistfully, more to herself than to me. "Our beginning was so wonderful. But in the end that beginning turns out to be a torture."

"Is it torture for you, too?"

"It's the sorrow I feel for you, sorrow because you have been too honest with me."

"I think honesty is an important part of true love," I said, a little defiantly.

Mom Ratchawong Kirati collected herself and continued quite normally. "If I'd done something to displease you at the outset, things wouldn't be this way."

"But I'm perfectly happy with my position at the moment. No matter how much pain love may cause us, it is a wonderful blessing in life, as you yourself said. I'm not wrong am I, in thinking that you love me in the same way I love you, with all my heart and soul?"

"Believe me, please, Nopphon, you must try to control your feelings."

Ultimately, I received no clear answer from her lips while we were together at Atami.

We stayed at the Osaka Hotel for two days. Mom Ratchawong Kirati and I scarcely had a chance to make our farewells alone. Early the following morning, which was the day we were to travel to Kobe, Mom Ratchawong Kirati knocked on the door of my room. When I opened the door, she seemed surprised to see me already dressed in a blue woolen suit with waistcoat and tie, instead of in my nightwear.

"I didn't think you'd be up yet, because we were late getting to bed last night. Why are you all dressed up and ready to go? We not leaving before nine o'clock."

"I know. But I couldn't sleep, so I got up and got dressed. And in a minute I think I'll go downstairs because I feel I need to get out."

"It's cooler today than it was, and there's a thick fog. I hope you're not going outside now."

"No, I'm not now." I closed the door and went and sat down on the chair in front of the desk which stood near the bed. Mom Ratchawong Kirati sat down on the edge of the bed. I was over-joyed to see her so early, even though I was a little puzzled as to why it was she wanted to see me at such an early hour.

In Mom Ratchawong Kirati's presence that morning, our last before we were to be parted, my heart pounded violently. I sat there, sadly, trying to compose myself. Mom Ratchawong Kirati did not utter a word. Thirty seconds passed in silence. Finally she spoke. "We're leaving Osaka between half past nine and ten o'clock. We'll have lunch at Kobe, at the invitation of a Thai friend there. The boat sails at two o'clock."

At the last sentence, my heart missed a beat.

"Once we get to Kobe, we're sure to get completely caught up in farewells. We won't get another chance to be alone," she added in the same measured tone. She paused for a moment. A lump rose in my throat. I avoided her eyes and blinked several times. "I thought you'd want at least ten minutes so that we could say our own farewells, so that's why I came to see you so early." Her voice was composed. It filled me with such pity.

"That's what I wanted so much. I'm most grateful to you for giving me this opportunity," I said, and then fell silent.

"You must get down to your studies so that you can achieve your ambitions. When I'm in Thailand, I'll pray for you."

"Please think of me all the time. Please understand me and the love I feel for you."

"I promise I will. Is there anything else, Nopphon?"

"I have a million more words to say, but time is short. I'd like to choose just a hundred that would make you understand that full million, but I can't find the right ones."

"Just say what you can. The rest I'll read in your eyes."

My eyes met hers and I felt even more gloomy. "Go ahead and read, then. I still don't know what to say."

We gazed into each other's eyes for a moment. Finally Mom Ratchawong Kirati got up and came and stood by my side. She put her hand on my shoulder and said, "My dear, please, for the last time, take my advice. You left your home and country and came to Japan to study, not to love me. Keep your target clearly in mind and stick to it. Forget what has been between us over the last two months. Think of it as a dream."

I took hold of her hand and stroked it gently. "This is real flesh and blood. This is really you. It's certainly no image nor shadow in a dream. How am I supposed to think of it as a dream? I love this flesh and blood so desperately."

Mom Ratchawong Kirati slowly withdrew her hand and turned her face away. "Chao Khun may wake soon. In a minute I must go back to my room. Our time is almost up my dear."

I rose to my feet. "Do you love me?" I asked, my voice scarcely more than a whisper.

"I'm your closest friend," Mom Ratchawong Kirati replied as she took off her silk scarf and handed it to me. "Please take this to remind you of me." She held out her hand to me. I could scarcely hold back my sadness and tears welled up in my eyes. I lifted her hand and kissed it. She made no protest.

Mom Ratchawong Kirati lowered her head and was silent for a moment. "I must go back to my room. We'll meet again in the dining room. Please keep your feelings under control." Having said this, she looked me straight in the eye and then turned round and walked slowly towards the door.

We arrived at the quayside at half past one. More than ten people, including both Thai and Japanese friends, had come to see Chao Khun and his wife off. We chatted together in a group in the saloon. I was not interested in any of them. All I did was glance over at Mom Ratchawong Kirati, so as to transfer the image of her face into the depths of my heart.

The end had arrived. The ship gave a blast on its whistle and a bell was sounded to warn friends and relatives to leave the vessel. Chao Khun and his wife bade farewell to all of their friends in the saloon. When they got round to me, Chao Khun shook my hand and thanked me at great length. "I shan't forget your kindness, young man. You've been most helpful to us."

I felt my heart miss a beat at his last sentence and I did not know what to say in reply. I was the last person that Mom Ratchawong Kirati said goodbye to. She held out her hand to me." Goodbye, my dear boy," she said, very quietly. Even so, her voice trembled and she hesitated, her lips pursed tightly.

"Please think of me always," I said.

"I will. Always. Goodbye."

"Goodbye." I gritted my teeth and had to make an effort to hold back my tears for the honor of the woman I so loved.

"Goodbye."

We followed the others out of the saloon. As we were about to leave the ship, Chao Khun became involved in another round of farewells. In the midst of this, I had a moment to be close to Mom Ratchawong Kirati some way apart from all the others. She held out her hand to me for the last time. "Do you love me?" I whispered, for the last time also.

"Hurry along now, Nopphon," she said, and then covered her face with her hand for a moment. "Hurry. I can't stand it." She bit her lower lip. I did likewise. Our eyes were filled with tears, but we each made a supreme effort to fight them back.

"Goodbye," I whispered finally. When I let go of her hand, I felt as if my heart had attached itself to her lovely palm.

—— THIRTEEN ——

When I realized that the woman I loved so much, with whom I had been both night and day, had gone far away, not just to a different district or different town, where I might take a cab or train to see her, but to another country, and that I was not in a position to overcome the obstacles to seeing her for a further five years, my grief and misery at such thoughts defied description.

On the train from Kobe to Tokyo, I felt torn apart when I thought of Mom Ratchawong Kirati. I traveled overnight, and how I thought of her, that night! When I reached Tokyo the next morning, I went straight to Aoyamachihan District to see her house. I felt as if I were visiting the grave of someone I loved dearly. It was as if Mom Ratchawong Kirati had died. The front gate, which was about chest height, was locked. I walked quietly round the outside of the grounds, recalling how we had sat here or walked there. The windows and doors of the house were all tightly shut and there was not a sound to be heard.

I sat down on a grassy mound beneath an overhanging vine on the spot where the two of us used to sit and chat in the evenings before Mom Ratchawong Kirati retired to bed. I could still remember her sweet yet penetrating gaze in the bright moonlit evenings. Often I felt disturbed when I looked into those wondrous eyes. How long I was there, lost in reveries of Mom Ratchawong Kirati, I do not remember. The weather that morning was cool and overcast with no sunshine nor sign of improvement. As I got up from the grass hillock and cast one more glance around the grounds of the house, I felt tears come to my eyes. I felt a sense of sadness and parting, even though it had only been a place where she had stayed.

I returned home, and after supper, instead of joining the rest of the family in the living room to listen to the radio, or gramaphone, or chat or read the newspaper, as I usually did, I excused myself and remained alone in my room. I was unable to join them in their relaxation because I felt for certain that I would be of no use to anyone. My mind was completely numb and I was preoccupied with just one thing.

I tried to find a way to relieve this obsession with Mom Ratchawong Kirati. I needed to find a way to unburden myself a little, instead of bottling up all my feelings inside to the point where things became unbearable. But there was no one I could talk to. I still retained sufficient sense not to tell anyone that I was madly in love with Mom Ratchawong Kirati, madly in love with a woman whose husband was my father's friend. I still had enough sense to realize that such an announcement would be damaging, both to myself and to the woman I loved. I certainly would not have received much in the way of sympathy.

There was only one way out, and that was to tell her how crazy I was about her. So that night I wrote a letter to Mom Ratchawong Kirati. What follows here, was that first letter.

My dear Khunying,

I almost went out of my mind as you drew away into the distance and I could no longer make out the beauty of your face. I almost collapsed on the quayside when that tiny hand could wave no more. I don't know how I got back to Tokyo. I returned that same night, feeling as dazed as if I were drunk. I couldn't get through another night without you unless I gave vent to my feelings. I miss you so much, it's driving me out of my mind. It's overwhelming me. I must unburden myself.

I can't swim across the seas to you, but I can reach you with this letter and beg you to listen to me one more time. This is no letter at all: it is a real person. When you reach home in Bangkok and take it out of the envelope, please don't think of it as something remote. It's your Nopphon. If you should kiss it just once, I shall feel the sweetness of that kiss, even though our bodies are thousands of miles apart.

As I write, you must have passed Moyi and now be beyond Japanese waters. I try to picture you in my mind. Perhaps you are sitting in the saloon, having just finished dinner. But I suspect you don't really want to be among a large group of people. You'll let Chao Khun chat with the Captain and the other passengers. You, yourself, perhaps, will go up on deck to be alone. In my mind I watch your movements . . . Tonight there is pale moonlight, but in the middle of the sea, there is nothing for you to cast your gaze upon except the ripple of the waves and the stars in the sky. Out there in the middle of the sea, the world is only sky and water. Why have you gone out up onto the deck? To think of me in peace, without being disturbed by anyone else? To think of home, in Bangkok? Or to enjoy the soft moonlight and cool breeze?

Oh, what a fool I am! Always my mind leads me into seeing your actions in such a way as to leave me feeling disturbed. But in actual fact, it would be most unlikely that you would stand out on deck in the breeze on a night like this. Even just off the islands of Japan, it would be too cold, and there would be no reason for you to stand out there alone in the cold like that.

If you were in the saloon, you'll probably be walking along the side of the boat, down below, where you don't have to face too strong a wind. Perhaps you're leaning over the railing at the stern, where it is shielded from the wind, looking down into the sea and thinking about me a little, or perhaps a lot. Your Nopphon is following you everywhere. I appear wherever you look. Can you see me there in the water? I am like the wake that follows a ship; that sparkle in the wash is the sparkle in my eyes. Can you see me?

If I could be granted one magical power, I would wish that I might be so transformed that I might enter your heart and know what you are thinking at all times, and how much you were thinking of your Nopphon. Surely it wouldn't be that you didn't think of me at all?

I've just realized one awful truth, and that is, although I tried to ask you numerous times, you never gave me an answer as to whether you loved me or not. I know that your silence was not an indication that you rejected my love. But I wanted so badly to hear you say it out clearly. If you were just to tell me you loved me, I would consider it the most wonderful blessing I had ever received in all my life. Can you grant me that wish I beg of you?

You've already assured me that you won't forget to think of me. But you should understand that I don't want you to think of me as a child you might take pity on or play along with. I want you to think of me as—what shall I say—can I say, the one you love most of all, or the only one you love? You may be wondering if I've gone out of my mind as I write this. I'm not sure either, whether a person who misses someone with every ounce of their feelings and says as much in all sincerity, is out of their mind or not.

I don't want to end this letter quickly, because I feel that while I am writing, our spirits are very close, and that makes me feel a little better, no matter how far away from me you are at present. But I don't know what else to write, because it would only be telling you how much I miss you all the time. So I should end my letter now and say goodnight. Oyasuminasai, my dear Khunying. Even sleep is something to be most grateful for. You can be sure I'll dream about you while I'm asleep.

With much love,
Nopphon

When I had finished the letter, I read it through several times. It was not to examine how elegantly I had written. It was not my intention to write a letter to Mom Ratchawong Kirati in which style was the important thing. The reason I reread it several times was to taste once again the sweet flavor of my feelings, which was enough to raise my spirits and ease my sorrow. I remember I went to sleep quite easily that night, I was so exhausted. I dreamt a hundred dreams, but they were all scenes from the same dream or of the same person.

I bore with my sorrow and loneliness for a few days and when I could stand it no longer, I wrote another letter to Mom Ratchawong Kirati, while she was still at sea.

—— FOURTEEN ——

A little over a month after Mom Ratchawong Kirati had left, I received a letter from her. My mind had been in turmoil for many days before I received the letter. Every afternoon when I returned home from the university, I would look at the letters in the mailbox, and when I did not find what I had been waiting for so anxiously, I would then have to go and ask other members of the household if there were any letter for me. I did this for so many days that it caused considerable surprise within the house, until the day finally came, when I received a letter from her.

I was feeling miserable that, as usual, there was no news from Mom Ratchawong Kirati. As I sat in front of the door taking off my shoes and feeling utterly lonely, Nobuko, the daughter of the owner of the house, ran up to me and handed me an envelope. I examined the handwriting on the front, and having ascertained whose hand it was, I kicked off my shoes absent-mindedly and in such a hurry as to startle Nobuko. All I wanted to do was rush to my room, close the door, lie down and relish the contents of the letter on my own. I thanked Nobuko briefly and went to my room, my face beaming of course. Mom Ratchawong Kirati's letter went as follows:

My dear Nopphon,

I've been home for five days now and have received your two letters. Although you wrote on different days, they both arrived together. In fact, I should have written to you without waiting to see if there was a letter from you because I needed to write to you straightaway to thank you for your most valuable assistance and the kindness you showed me throughout my stay in Tokyo. The one thing I won't thank you for, is for taking too much interest in me.

I didn't expect to get a letter from you so quickly. I suppose you'll be angry with me for not writing sooner. Or is it that you you were too quick in writing to me? If I walk but you fly, you can't really compare, can you? I hope you won't be angry with me. However, I've done a good deed in return, and that is, I'm writing this letter the day after receiv-ing yours. I'm sure you won't be so hasty as to say I ought to have answered on the very same day. If you do get rather im-patient, please don't forget the fact that at home in Bangkok, I'm not free like you. I have lots of different jobs I have to do, which is something you possibly never realized.

The ardor that you expressed in your last letter suggests, I think, that the significance of the end of autumn has not yet touched your heart. It was as if you had sneaked into Bangkok to write that letter. If you still haven't cooled down, I'm going to have to advise you to stay in an icebox when you write to me next time. Or else you could wait until winter and write from somewhere where it's snowing. I say this, not because I am treating your letter as something amusing; I feel for you so much, so very much. But I know this madness will make you unhappy. I want you to be happy, no matter what.

On the journey home, I didn't feel particularly excited. I didn't eagerly count off the hours and days, as many do when they've been away from their homeland. Perhaps it was because I'd only been away a few months. Another thing was, there was no one in Bangkok whom I thought of every hour of every day. I missed my father and sisters, but not that much—just ordinarily. But in leaving you, I have to admit that my mind was hardly at peace. I knew my departure would leave you alone and upset for many days. The feelings you describe in your letters were scarcely more than I feared. All I hope is that you can keep them under control. Your intense feelings for me will gradually disappear in due course and eventually, I will cease to occupy a significant place in your life. Then happiness and innocence will return once more to your heart without the fetters of being a young man. I'm waiting and praying for that day.

Do you realize, the way you described your feelings in those two letters has made you into a man I need to be wary of? You're no longer my sweet young friend, Nopphon. Your childlike charm has almost completely disappeared and you seem to have become quite a terrifying young man. From your letters I can scarcely recognize the Nopphon I first met. You must, my dear young friend, I beg you, try to come to your senses. You must keep your feelings firmly under control. You have the strength to do so if you try. It would be so tragic for you to be infatuated with such an unfortuante woman, long since abandoned by fortune, and even now, not in a position to fulfill anyone's dreams. Even though people would forgive you for your infatuation with the woman, you have to admit that this obsession is really meaningless. What point is there in being so obsessed with me when your desire has no chance of being realized? Is it the ocean that keeps me from you? Surely you know it's because I have Chao Khun that we are parted and live in separate worlds. There's no way we can come together, you know full well, don't you?

Nopphon, why do you still dream of me? I can't help you. There's no one in this world who can help you. Life runs its course, that's true, but the gods have already paved it out in advance. I neither ask you, nor forbid you to think of me. But I do ask that you think of me calmly, like a close friend, or an older sister. What I don't want, is for you to become too emotionally worked up. Please don't think of me with the desire to seize my body and soul as your treasures. You already know that is impossible. Please return to where you were, my dear young friend, to your books and dreams of a married life of honor and prosperity. You have a brighter, more wonderful future than that woman who merely crossed the path of your life for a brief while. Please let me hope that my warning might have some effect.

I ask you to work hard at your studies. That is your only goal now. I, for one, shall always be interested in your success. My pleasure at wishing you a future full of great honor and prosperity, will be second to none, if I live that long. I wait eagerly for the day when there will be news that your feelings have returned to normal. I hope that such a time will come very soon, and from that day, I shall be happy and contented.

Although this letter is filled only with requests, I am certainly not going to forget to tell you that I accept your worthy feelings with pleasure and deep gratitude. I will remember them forever. There's no need for you to say it again. Think of me, my dear, think of me just a little from time to time.

I've already written at great length, so I hope you'll forgive me if I don't write about anyone else in this letter. But let me chide you a little, for not writing to Chao Khun. Do you realize how careless it was to be only interested in writing to me? I nearly had a fright when Chao Khun asked me what you had said in your letter. If you'd been there at the time, I'm sure you'd have really been in a panic. Luckily he's not the jealous type and I'm not easily alarmed. Can I finish now, my dear? Chao Khun is getting ready for bed and I don't want him to go asking questions unnecessarily. Goodbye, my young friend. I think of you constantly. I shall always.

> With concern for your happiness,
> Kirati

This first letter from Mom Ratchawong Kirati eased my agitated mind considerably. Her words cheered me up as much as if I had met her and heard them from her own lips. At first I saw no point in her advice. I took no notice, regarding it merely as words of consolation. She could not really have meant that I should cease to think of her so passionately. But later, after I had read her letter again and reflected upon it, I was inclined to think that there was something in her advice. Perhaps Mom Ratchawong Kirati really did mean it.

——— FIFTEEN ———

After that, Mom Ratchawong Kirati and I continued to write to each other. As time passed, the pain of missing her, for several reasons, gradually diminished. In the first place, however much I loved her and however much I missed her, there was nothing I could do about it. Soon the tension I had felt, began to ease. Another factor was that when the time came for me to devote my time to my studies, I had to use all of my powers of concentration, which brought my mind back from the realms of passionate love to its former state.

Having suppressed my feelings once, it seemed as if I could do so perpetually. Following the first two letters which were filled with an outpouring of love and passion for her, I continued in the next few letters to describe my longing for her. But when I considered Mom Ratchawong Kirati's advice and the utter emotional exhaustion I had experienced when she first left, my passion eased of its own accord. Thus, in subsequent letters I made no mention of longing for her, as I had at the beginning, and the interval between writing grew longer until the time came when my mind had reached its former equilibrium. Writing to her became almost completely painless and might even have been described as writing simply to a close friend. And that was the way Mom Ratchawong Kirati wished it, as I understood at the time.

I had told her of my love and begged her in several letters to answer me in just one word. But no matter how pleasing her replies were, she never ever mentioned love. This was another major reason for making me think that Mom Ratchawong Kirati really did want me to forget what was between us, or at least, the incident on Mount Mitake, where I had allowed my feelings to gush forth before her and had pressed my lips up against hers. That kiss still simmered in my heart. I had not forgotten it. Yet the memory was beginning to fade for the various reasons I have already mentioned.

After two years, communication between Mom Ratchawong Kirati and myself had become so infrequent that scarcely a trace of the past remained in my heart. Letters, which I had written to her every month, without fail, became less frequent, and it seems that in that second year, I wrote to her only three times. In fact, I was increasingly burdened with my studies, and as I had recovered my mental equilibrium, I immersed myself in my studies and plans for my future career. Looking back at the way I felt then, I, myself, am still surprised and at a loss to explain why Mom Ratchawong Kirati so quickly lost importance to me. I had been so besotted with her and regarded her as the most important person in my life. She was a woman I could not separate from my own life, because if she were separated from it, my life would no longer have been complete. After the passage of two years, all I knew was that she was just one of many close friends I had in Bangkok.

About six months later, I received news from Mom Ratchawong Kirati that Chao Khun had passed away as a result of kidney disease. I shared her sorrow at hearing the news and quickly wrote back offering my condolences. After that life went on as usual. Chao Khun's death did not for one moment prompt me to consider that I might become involved in Mom Ratchawong Kirati's life in a way that might be significant both to her life and my own. It should have made me think of the former relationship between us once more. It should have done, it is true, but I do not know what devil it was that blocked it from my mind. It is most surprising that, having learned the news of Chao Khun's death, I allowed things to carry on as usual. I had no inkling that an event of little significance to me was of the utmost importance to the life of someone else. Such is life.

I continued my studies for a further two years and successfully completed them. As I drew near to finishing, I had more contact with my family in Bangkok. My brothers and sisters, who had heard I was doing well and would soon be finishing and returning home, all wrote to express their delight; so too, did the girl I was engaged to. Father must surely have suggested she write, as a means of tying me down and warning me that there was already a girl waiting to marry me in Bangkok and that I should not go getting involved with any other women in Japan. Truly, no one need have worried about me on that score. At the time, I was more preoccupied with the progress of my own career than anything else. I was not going to waste my time on any women. I had hardly given a thought even to my own fiancée. I had no time for such things. I was older now, it was true; but this had not focused my thoughts on choosing a spouse. It seemed that the older I got, the more I kept away from the female sex; indeed, now I was mature, I avoided all other situations and concentrated entirely on my work.

The letter from my fiancée disturbed my peace of mind and turned my thoughts to marriage. But it was not something I considered with any great excitement. I did not know whether I would love her, because we did not know each other well enough to be able to be fully committed in love. But then what was marriage? I was not very clear about it at the time. I thought vaguely that she must be a suitable enough partner. Otherwise, why would my father have chosen her to be my spouse, for he was no fool. At a suitable time after my return to Bangkok, he would probably arrange our marriage and I would raise no objections. Even though the marriage would not be built upon a basis of mutual love, I would gradually become close to her and before long would feel fondness and love for her. She would look after the home and I would go to work and struggle against all difficulties for advancement in my career. There was not much more to marriage than this. That was the rather vague idea I had at the time. I did not think about it very seriously. I wrote a friendly letter back to her.

When I finished my studies, instead of returning home im-mediately, I began training at a bank. During that time I wrote to Mom Ratchawong Kirati, telling her how I was getting on. I did not write at any length, for the truth was, latterly, I was no longer very good at writing her long letters. Once I had said what I wanted to, I could hardly think of anything else to write. How strangely time changes our feelings.

So that you will know how Mom Ratchawong Kirati felt about me, four years after we had parted, I would like to show you one of her letters of the time. "My dear Nopphon"—*that was how she always, without fail, began her letters. This is how she goes on:*

I have received your letter telling me of your success. How can I tell you how thoroughly delighted I am! If you had an elder sister, her pleasure at your success would scarcely compare with that which I feel. You know just how eager I have been for you to succeed throughout the many long years when we have not seen each other. So if I boast of my happiness a little too much, even though I'm not exaggerat-ing, you surely won't be cross with me.

I'm even more delighted to learn that you're going to stay over there and work for a year before returning to Thailand. In fact, that was your original plan, I was told when I went to Tokyo, and so it just proves how strong your deter-mination is.

I expect you show the same determination in everything, not just your studies. Though the achievements of people like you may be beyond other people, they are well within your capacity. My praise is meant quite sincerely.

Another year until you come to Thailand and we meet again. You'll no longer be the young Nopphon I used to know. It will have been almost six years since we parted. You were twenty-two then, so you'll be twenty-eight. My Nop-phon will be quite grown up, no longer a boy like before. You're bound to be very different; but it will be the difference which comes with maturing and thriving. Quite the opposite to me, whom you will also think different; but different in the sense of decaying. However, we'll surely recognize each other because we share certain memories we can never forget.

It's strange how, latterly, contact between us has become so infrequent. Two years ago, I still remember, I didn't hear from you more than three times throughout the year. But in fact, it was my own wish that you should have all your time for studying without having to worry about regularly writing letters back and forth, so what you did, was correct.

Nearly five years have passed without any great hardship. One year will go much more quickly and smoothly. I haven't any further words of advice because you are your own master and it looks as if you can manage even better than me. I await your return, my dear, to see with my own eyes the progress in life my young friend has made.

> Thinking of you always,
> Kirati

I read her letter with no emotion. Of course I felt a sense of gratitude towards her, as if she were my older sister. She had given me advice and encouragement which had always been of great value to me. But the feeling of passion had died. Time had swept away my infatuation for her without me realizing it. I did not notice, nor was I aware, that Mom Ratchawong Kirati had concealed the depth of her feelings in that letter. Subtlety and discretion were, at that time, beyond my comprehension.

—— SIXTEEN ——

There were few people on the Mitsui Bussan Company's wharf on the morning when the vessel, *Nachisanmaru* brought me in to Bangkok from Japan. This was because there were no more than seven or eight passengers on the boat, of whom I was the only Thai. Thus, when the boat came alongside, I was able to see quite clearly the group of people waiting to meet me.

The first person I saw was my father. He was standing at the front of a group of more than ten close relatives. There were four or five close friends of about the same age as me there, too. Among the group of relatives was a woman I did not recognize, but from the way she looked at me, she seemed every bit as interested in me as anyone else.

I saw no sign of Mom Ratchawong Kirati among the group. Only when I cast my eyes around the whole compound did I see a beautiful figure in a navy blue suit, leaning back against the door of a large saloon car. Then I saw the tiny hand waving slowly to me. I waved back happily, because even though she was standing some distance away, I recognized the figure as Mom Ratchawong Kirati.

Once the crew had fixed the gangway, all the friends and relatives who had come to meet me boarded the boat. I stood by the gangway, ready to greet them. My father was the first to welcome me. He came straight up to me and hugged his eldest son with all the love and emotion which had been bottled up for eight years. I hugged him with the same feelings, and then other relatives and friends crowded round and showed their feelings in a similar fashion. I cannot describe how I felt that first morning I reached Bangkok. It was the most wonderful day of my life, and never since have I experienced such joy and happiness.

As I was greeting one lady a little uncertainly, my father came across and placed his hand on my shoulder and told me that this was my fiancée. Then I recognized her. She had a plain, ordinary-looking face, neither ugly, nor beautiful. Standing before me, her manner was one of shyness and embarrassment. I am not good at making conversation and since we were only slightly acquaint-ed, I said only a few words, and then she retired to let others come and greet me.

Mom Ratchawong Kirati was the last to come and see me. She was wearing a navy blue outfit with a white floral pattern. It was the same color she had been wearing when I first met her in Tokyo, five or six years earlier. However, even though they were the same clothes that I remember from a long time back when we first met, surprisingly, that morning, it did not strike me. It was surprising, too, that Mom Ratchawong Kirati should come to meet me on my first day in Bangkok, wearing the same clothes that she had worn six years ago. Her manner was still calm and graceful, as before. The only difference was that she was even more graceful with the dignity of her age, which was now approaching forty-one. Although she had lost a little of her radiance, her charm and great beauty had not abandoned her. She was still striking in appearance.

Mom Ratchawong Kirati touched my hand and I squeezed hers with all the joy and excitement I would have felt at meeting a sister who had been away a long time. I was the first to speak.

"I've missed you a lot."

"I've thought of you often, ever since we parted," she said slowly and calmly, although I could clearly see the deep happi-ness in her eyes. I felt embarrassed by her words when I recalled that no matter how intensely I had missed her on occasions, my feelings had not remained constant, as hers had for me.

"I'm so pleased to see you again," I continued.

"And I've been waiting for you. Waiting all the time."

"You're so kind to me."

"If what you say is true, then so I should be, shouldn't I?"

"I fear I'm not worthy. You're too kind to me," I said laughing. I paid no attention to the effect my response might have upon Mom Ratchawong Kirati. Nevertheless, she was silent for a while.

"You're hurting my hand," Mom Ratchawong Kirati said gently. "Today isn't like when we parted at the port of Kobe."

"Oh, I'm sorry," I cried, releasing her hand immediately. "It's Bangkok now, and we don't have to part again. We don't have to go through such misery again."

"Who knows, Nopphon?" she countered softly, which surprised me a little.

"Well, I'm not planning to leave here again for the rest of my life."

"But that's not the only cause of parting, nor the only source of sorrow," she said, touching my arm. "But let's not argue about it now. All your relations are wanting you."

"You're as much a relation to me."

"That may be so. That may be so. But I still shouldn't keep you to myself today. Off you go, my dear, go and see your father."

So together, we went straight to the saloon where most of my friends and relations were waiting. Some of them dragged me off to the cabin I had occupied at sea, to see what my living con-ditions were like and to help carry my things down off the boat. After that, I was constantly surrounded by people and scarcely got another opportunity to speak to Mom Ratchawong Kirati.

As we disembarked, I invited her to continue our conversation at home.

"I must excuse myself, Nopphon. You should spend all of your first day with your close relatives."

"No relative is going to want me for the whole day."

"Well, there's your father, at least. He's going to want several hours to chat with a son who's been away for seven or eight years. And there are others, too."

"My father's not going to be so desperate as to say everything in one single day," I replied with a laugh. Even so, my manner remained composed.

"Let's meet another day, Nopphon."

"In that case, I'll visit you as soon as I can, " I said, deferring to her wishes.

The curtain fell all too quickly and unremarkably on that first day's meeting in Bangkok between Mom Ratchawong Kirati and myself. Most of that day was taken up with meeting people, with a short rest in the afternoon. In the evening, after dinner, I talked with my father in the sitting room. At one point in our long conversation the subject of Mom Ratchawong Kirati came up.

"So you're very well acquainted with Khunying Atthikan, are you?" he asked, as we chatted casually about one thing and another.

"You mean Khunying Kirati? Yes," I continued, when he had confirmed this, "we're good friends. When she was in Japan, I was with Chao Khun and her, visiting them and helping them nearly all the time."

"It's a shame Chao Khun Atthikan died so soon. When he was alive," my father continued, "I heard him speak very highly indeed of his wife, and from what I've seen since he died, I think she's a lovely woman, well worthy of high regard."

"I have great admiration for her," I responded. "Even though it wasn't very long, I got to know her very well. I've never met anyone as intelligent as her. I think she ought to marry again. And surely she won't be able to escape the intentions of some-one."

"I'm not so sure, because since the death of Chao Khun Atthikan, I've heard that she takes little pleasure in society. She leads a quiet life and is held in high esteem by all of Chao Khun Atthikan's close friends everywhere. Recently I heard that there was someone paying her a lot of attention, even, it seems, to the point of sounding her out on marriage. But she turned him down. People say she seems like someone hiding some secret."

I listened calmly in silence and after that my father changed the subject.

—— SEVENTEEN ——

About five days after my arrival in Bangkok, I found a convenient time to pay Mom Ratchawong Kirati a visit. In fact, it was somewhat belated. I should have gone to see her much sooner, but I had several urgent matters to settle, largely concern-ing my career, which, at that time, preoccupied my thoughts above all else.

I went to visit her at her home in Bangkapi. It was a modest bungalow set in about three *rai* of grounds, surrounded by a thick hedge of morning glory, with its green leaves and purple flowers.

The house stood back some way, clearly visible on elevated ground. To the left was a large pond, and near a gate, a small pavilion standing among the flower beds, with creeping plants growing all over it. It made a pleasing sight.

My first impression when I reached Mom Ratchawong Kirati's house, was that compared with the dozen or so I had passed on the way, it was one of the nicest in Bangkapi. They were all lovely houses, but the setting and layout of the grounds were not as pleasant and as soothing as Mom Ratchawong Kirati's home. Looking at the flower beds, which in places included large stones, I felt as if I had known this house for a long time. This was because of the way the garden was laid out, which was very similar to the Japanese style. Different types of plants had not been arranged in strict groups but were all mixed together. They grew in a dense mass, making the garden look natural, rather than one that had been created. And even though it had in fact been deliberately created, it seemed as natural as the magnificent gardens at Nikko, which I had visited so often.

The gate was already open. The car passed slowly through and as I looked among the flowers, I saw a woman's head appear by the orange jasmine bush. I recognized the hairstyle and ordered the car to stop before it reached the building. As I got out and stood there on the path, Mom Ratchawong Kirati appeared from the bushes and came into full sight.

"Nopphon," she called from the distance.

I raised my hat to her and took a short cut over towards her. As soon as I reached her, an Alsatian, which had been playing nearby, ran up and stood right up against me, eyeing me fiercely. She bent over and patted it gently on the head. Then she called its name two or three times and it lay down quietly at her feet.

"That's a large and very frightening dog you've got," I began. "It's eyeing me suspiciously."

She smiled. "Thorwald is my bodyguard. There aren't many people living here, so we have to rely on Thorwald as our watchman. You're right, though. Thorwald is suspicious of everyone at first. I've explained to him now that you're my friend and you mean no harm." As she finished speaking, Mom Ratchawong Kirati patted Thorwald on the head and told him to run along and play somewhere else. He did as he was told.

"I should be receiving you inside," she continued, looking up. We were standing by a garden table which had been placed among the flower beds and which was where Mom Ratchawong Kirati had been sitting before.

"I really like it here," I said, putting my hat down on the table. "It's nice and cool, and it looks lovely with all these different kinds of flowers."

"If you like, then, I'll receive you here."

"I must apologize," I said, when we were both seated, "for not coming to see you sooner. It was because I had to go and see lots of important people about my job. I didn't want to waste any time."

"I think it's quite right, Nopphon, that you should think of your work before anything else."

"I have to confess that over the last two or three years I've been really preoccupied with the thought of work. It's not that I want money to satisfy any cravings for pleasure. The main reason is I want to work. I believe it will give me great satisfaction if I can use the knowledge I gained from my studies in my work. It's this which might have left me deficient in certain other areas, such as socializing and, for example, coming to see you."

"It's a deficiency which makes you even nicer," she said with a smile. It was a smile of such tenderness and sweetness, a smile I had known long ago and which I recognized when I encountered it once more.

"You've really grown up, now, Nopphon. Do you realize, there's scarcely a trace of a boy left in you?"

"I suppose I must have changed. But it's not something I'm really aware of myself."

"You're a fine young man and you seem more serious than you were."

"I hadn't realized that. But as far as you're concerned, I see only a slight change."

"I've aged a lot."

"Well I don't think so. I beg your pardon, but how old are you?"

"Over forty."

"Well, I beg your pardon, but you still look very young . . ."

"What is all this, Nopphon? Aren't you going to stop saying, 'I beg your pardon'?" There was irritation in her voice. "You sound as if I were always blaming you for everything. You really do seem to have changed a lot."

"I was afraid I might be saying something I shouldn't."

"Even so, there's no need to apologize when you've already said it. I'm not the woman you met in Tokyo. Nearly six years have passed since then. Unless you decide to flatter me too much, you can't say I still look young."

"But that's my honest opinion."

"You're too biased, believe me, Nopphon. I'm over forty now. I'm well aware that I've aged a lot."

"It may be that you're more biased than me," I remarked and then changed the subject. "You must like it here, in this house. It's beautiful, just right for you. Please tell me what's been happening to you."

She looked at me doubtfully.

"Do you think you're really still interested in what's been happening to me?"

"I've always been interested."

"Now that you've returned to Bangkok, and there is work and lots of friends you have to give your time to, I fear you may have very little time to be interested in what's been happening to me. Things are very different from when we met in Tokyo, aren't they, Nopphon?"

I was inclined to agree with what Mom Ratchawong Kirati had said. I had neither the time, nor the extravagant feelings to think of her in the same way as before. Episodes from the past had faded from my memory. Even the incident on Mount Mitake, which I had once thought such a momentous event in my life, I now scarcely ever thought about. It all seemed to belong to the past, as if it had come from a time of its own. The new era which had begun in my life was a period for work and my immediate livelihood. The truth was, there were no deep or strong feelings in my life like those that had been awakened six years ago. As for Mom Ratchawong Kirati, I could not work out whether she had said this purely out of a desire to express her true feelings or for some other reason. I did not know whether she, too, had entered a new phase of life, or not.

"I think I'm sufficiently interested in you to hear what's been happening to you," I said, thinking this a suitable response.

"All right, I'll tell you, as an old friend, without thinking about what you might be now," Mom Ratchawong Kirati said seriously. She paused for a moment to gather her thoughts. "I should begin after the death of Chao Khun. Just talking about his illness is so upsetting and I seem to have written to you about it already," she said slowly and thoughtfully. "Nor do I want to talk about how sad I felt after his death. I'll tell you about the main things that have happened to me. In the first place, he made me wealthier, by passing on to me about a third of his fortune in his will. The other two thirds went to his two children. In fact, I didn't expect to get a share, because I'd only lived with him for two or three years, and we had no children. Such kind-ness towards me leaves me wondering whether I really deserved it. Nopphon, do you think I'm lucky or unlucky?"

"That's a difficult question to answer," I replied cautiously.

"Exactly. I think it's a difficult question to answer, too." As she spoke, her eyes drifted into a reverie. "I had less than three years of married life before my husband died. Then I became wealthy, but at the same time, I have to live alone. Life's strange, isn't it, Nopphon?"

"Why didn't you go back and live with your father?"

"I'd lived with him for thirty-five years already. I love him dearly and I go to visit him and stay with him frequently. But I wouldn't go back to that kind of life. It was a life which con-demned me to such misfortune, emptiness, and bitterness, such as I'll never forget for the rest of my life."

"In that case, you should opt for getting out and about and meeting people."

"Indeed, I should. But I haven't." She spoke as if she had some doubts about her decision. "I'll tell you my story briefly. After Chao Khun died, I came to live here. Our old house passed on to his eldest son. I had no wish to continue living there, for one thing because it was too big, and for another, because it would have been a constant reminder that Chao Khun had gone forever. Chao Khun had bought this plot of land several years before his death, and we used to say we'd build a little holiday home here. After he died, I set about having it done as we had planned. The only difference is, instead of it being a place to stay temporarily, it's my permanent home."

"And it ought to be a house that brings great pleasure to its owner," I added, when she paused momentarily.

"It ought to," she said looking around the grounds with satisfaction. "Everyone who comes here says how nice my home is and expresses envy at the peace and quiet I have. But I'm not sure whether they're right or not."

"Besides this lovely house, what else do you have to keep you happy?"

"You still can't stop asking questions," Mom Ratchawong Kirati said with an indulgent smile. "That may be all that's left of the Nopphon I knew in Tokyo."

"Am I asking too much?" I inquired politely.

"No, not too much. But very few people would have asked me that. You're good at thinking up questions, because even I don't seem to have ever given a thought to what I have to keep me happy." She paused in thought for a moment and then added, "When I think about it, I can't help feeling surprised at myself, because my greatest happiness in the past, instead of being something real which had happened to me, was merely a hope, or anticipation of something. My life now is no different. Real happiness drifts along before me, while I follow along behind, snatching wildly at it, waiting and hoping."

"It seems like an exhausting life," I remarked sympathetically.

"What can I do, Nopphon? The powers that be in this world have determined that my life shall be so. No matter how I struggle, I can't escape, so I have to face up to my fate. Your life is worth much more than mine and it runs a much smoother course. In yours, there are only real things. You gain pleasure from events that happened in the past and then forget them completely and move on to new experiences and new pleasures. That's the way it goes, constantly changing. My life is confused with fading dreams and memories. Sometimes there is happiness, but it is not something clear and definite. It's like a mistake. Sometimes I enjoy myself, sometimes I feel worn out. That's the way my life is and what I intended to tell you. But it would be hard for you to understand."

"It's a strange, sad life and it's not easy to understand either," I murmured sincerely. "Now that you're well off, why don't you use your wealth to make your hopes come true. Then you'd be happy."

"Money is powerful, it's true, Nopphon, but it's not every-thing. It happens that what I have been hoping for and anti-cipating is not something that can be obtained by the power of money. This is my great misfortune." At this point, Mom Ratchawong Kirati got up. "There you are, Nopphon, let me finish my story there. It's more boring than interesting. I want to hear about you, now. We'll take a little walk and while we're doing so, please tell me what you've been doing. After that, we'll go in-side and I hope you'll stay and have dinner with me this evening, so I'll have the chance to hear about everything in detail."

I did as she asked. We did not have much time for a walk before dusk fell. As we walked side by side through the extensive gardens, there was nothing to interrupt the mood. We were alone together in the stillness with an atmosphere which ought to have evoked the intense feelings of six years ago. But surprisingly, my feelings were not in the least affected. It was not that Mom Ratchawong Kirati had lost her former charm and beauty. Indeed, I could still recognize these quite clearly. But it was with admiration rather, and with no emotional involvement on my part.

I stayed to dinner and talked with her until nine o'clock when I left. She told me she lived with an aunt and a niece, but as it happened, they had both gone to visit relatives that day and would perhaps stay overnight with them. Thus it was, that I spent altogether four hours alone with Mom Ratchawong Kirati. I enjoyed myself all the time I was with her, telling her about what I had been doing and listening to what had been happening to her, without a moment's boredom. At the dining table the two of us ate and chatted beneath a bright lamp for over an hour. I noticed that Mom Ratchawong Kirati's forty years were beginning to show in the wrinkles that appeared in places on her beautiful skin. But in her manner and conversation, she had not changed at all from the Mom Ratchawong Kirati of old. She was as sweet and graceful as ever. While she was busy serving out this and that, I could not help recalling the kindness she had showed me in the past. Yet all I recalled was that she was like an older sister to me. My feelings were not set into passionate turmoil as they once had been.

Throughout those four hours, I could not fathom out what aim Mom Ratchawong Kirati had in life.

—— EIGHTEEN ——

Because I was occupied with work, two months or so passed before I went to visit her again. My father had informed me that he had made arrangements for my wedding to take place in three months time. When I knew the date of the wedding, I thought it my duty to inform Mom Ratchawong Kirati as a matter of courtesy. On my second visit, she received me in the living room, but even so, there was no one to disturb us or interrupt our conversation.

Although Mom Ratchawong Kirati had not intended to show her disappointment at the interval of two months I had allowed to pass between my first and second visits, I could see clearly from the very beginning of our conversation just how dis-appointed and saddened she felt when I behaved differently to what she had expected. However, I myself, was unaware of the cause of such feelings. Whether it was because her feelings for me were more than I had realized, or what, it was beyond my comprehension.

Despite what I noticed about Mom Ratchawong Kirati's feelings, I made no reference to the matter, as I had no wish to make excuses for not seeing her very often because of being tied up with one thing or another. Such excuses might merely have served to make her feel more bitter, so I kept quiet that I was aware of her disappointment. After we had talked about various things for a while, I brought up the matter I had come to tell her about.

"I've got some news to tell you, Khunying."

"I hope it's very good news for you. It must be to do with some advancement in your work." She waited for my reply with interest.

"No. It is good news, but nothing to do with work. I'm sure you'd be pleased if I were to be getting married soon." I noticed that she looked slightly stunned, perhaps because she was not expecting such news.

"You're getting married?" she repeated uncertainly. "It's the lady who went to meet you the day you arrived in Bangkok, isn't it?"

"Oh, so you knew about us all along, then?"

"No, I had no idea. I just guessed. Have you known each other long?"

"She's my fiancée."

"Since when?" Instead of glowing with happiness, Mom Ratchawong Kirati's expression was full of doubt.

"Seven or eight years ago. A little before I left for Japan."

"But all the time I knew you in Tokyo, you never said a thing about your fiancée to me." Her voice registered even more doubt.

"Maybe that was because I wasn't in the least bit interested in the engagement myself."

"And now you've resigned yourself to marrying a lady whom you've never been interested in."

"It's my father's wish and I have no objections. Actually, she's an educated lady from a suitable background. Marriage will give my life a more solid base than I have at present."

Mom Ratchawong Kirati gazed at me for a moment before she spoke, with a look that was difficult to interpret. "You haven't told me your fiancée's name yet."

"It's Pari. Pari Buranawat."

"A pretty girl with a pretty name." She smiled in an absent-minded and uncertain manner. "I do congratulate you."

She held out her hand to me, and at the same time, I said, "You're the first to congratulate me."

"I regard that as a great honor," she replied modestly. We were both silent for a while, during which time I could not think of anything to say to her. Mom Ratchawong Kirati spoke first.

"What are your ideals in marriage?"

"I'm at a bit of a loss for an answer. I'm not very good at deal-ing with that kind of question."

"You used to ask me all kinds of detailed questions and I never tried to get out of them, so now, when it's my turn, you can't either."

"I wasn't thinking of getting out of it. But I'm afraid I have no ideals in marriage, to speak of."

"I'm surprised you say you have none," said Mom Ratchawong Kirati with a sigh. "Are all men like you, Nopphon?"

"Not all men. But maybe most of them." I said what I thought. "Men probably have ideals connected with their work more than anything else. Like me, for example."

"Do you love your fiancée?"

"We haven't known each other long. We both like each other well enough, and I hope we'll be able to love each other when we're married."

"Isn't love necessary for young people, then, before they decide to commit themselves to marriage?" Her question was filled with surprise. "All I've ever heard is, 'Love, but don't get married,' but here you are, Nopphon, getting married, and loving after-wards."

"If there were mutual love before marriage, it would be even better. However, I think that love is too complicated and too painful."

"What's made you see love in that light?"

"Because once I loved someone."

"Please tell me all about it." Mom Ratchawong Kirati's eyes began to sparkle.

"You already know all the details. It happened when you went to Japan and carried on until you left me and returned to Bang-kok. At first, love brought happiness, but it ended in pain and suffering. Later on, I thought that I had allowed myself to be carried away by my feelings in a very inappropriate way. I should have loved and respected you as an older sister. I realized that I had behaved very wrongly. Ever since, I've tried to completely forget the events of that time. And at that time, too, I learned just how much pain and torture such passionate love causes. I believe I'll never love like that again."

Mom Ratchawong Kirati gazed ahead with a distant look in her eyes. She said nothing.

"I didn't think I'd ever talk about this with you again," I said. "It makes me feel ashamed and despise myself."

"People have different ideas about love, but I agree with you that love crushes and tortures our hearts, sometimes more than we can stand. You did the right thing, like everyone else who is able to escape from the torture and forget the past. But some fools may be incapable of doing as you did. Let me congratulate you once again."

She paused for a while and her eyes avoided mine. When she turned to face me again, she asked, "Have you fixed a date?"

"My father said in about three months' time."

"Let me offer my best wishes in advance. I believe in love, so I shall wish that the two of you will love each other, whether before or after you marry, and that you will love each other deep-ly and within a short time." She picked up the teacup in front of her and raised it rather vigorously, smiling brightly as she added, "I drink to you, my dear friend, and to the love and happiness of the pair of you." She took a sip from the cup and then put it down. "I'll be the first to give any help at your wedding," she added.

After we had been talking for some time, I noticed that she was not very well, but she seemed to be trying to hide it, so as to appear to me perfectly happy and cheerful. I did not let on that I had noticed, but simply hastened to take leave of her on the grounds that I had business to attend to. Even so, I had been talking to her for almost two hours. I was sorry that I had brought such important news at a time when she was not very well. Under normal circumstances, Mom Ratchawong Kirati would have shown much greater excitement and pleasure, and would not have allowed me to leave so quickly, that is for sure. Those were my thoughts at the time.

—— NINETEEN ——

I never, for one moment, dreamt that that visit to Mom Ratcha-wong Kirati would be the opening of the final scene in her life. How cruel it was, that this scene should have drawn to an end so quickly.

The marriage between myself and Pari, my fiancée, took place on the appointed day. I shall not go into details about the scale and splendor of our wedding. What did leave me feeling dis-appointed, was that Mom Ratchawong Kirati did not come to the wedding. She sent someone round with a letter in the after-noon, to say she was ill and would not be able to attend. She sent her best wishes and said she would come and visit me when she was feeling better.

I had already planned to take my wife on holiday to Hua Hin for a fortnight. Before going down there, I took her to visit Mom Ratchawong Kirati at her home. This was three days after the wedding. Mom Ratchawong Kirati told us she was feeling a bit better and was planning to pay us a visit in the near future. I could see quite clearly that she looked paler than before. When asked about her condition, she said she felt weak, but that on our wedding day, she had had a fever, too. She looked drowsy and did not say very much. She asked us to tell her about our wedding day, and listened in silence, except for the occasional question, and to ask Pari how she had felt on the day. I spent about an hour with her and then left, fearing she might not enjoy our visit, as she was not yet back to normal health.

"She's a sweet lady, and still beautiful," Pari remarked, once we were outside. "But there does seem something a little mysterious about her."

Two months passed. One evening in December, a startling incident and revelation of love occurred. That evening, I return-ed home from work, and before I had time to change my clothes, a servant came and told me there was a lady waiting to see me urgently. I hurried down to meet her in the living room. It was Mom Ratchawong Kirati's aunt, who was waiting there for me with an anxious look on her face.

"You wanted to see me urgently," I began.

"Khunying is seriously ill," she said.

"Last time I saw her, she was getting better, wasn't she?" I asked with a mixture of surprise and alarm. "What's the matter with her now?"

She told me that Mom Ratchawong Kirati had had mild tuberculosis for about two years. Previously, it had been understood that if she were well cared for, the condition would not suddenly worsen, to the point where her life might be in danger, and that there was hope that she might get better. But in the last couple of months, the course of her illness had changed, and in the last two or three days, her condition had deteriorated alarmingly. She had a raging fever and was frequently delirious, during which times she would talk of her trip to Japan with her husband, Chao Khun, often mentioning my name.

"Whenever anyone comes to visit her, before I even have a chance to tell her who it is, she always asks if it's Nopphon. That's what she asks when she's fully conscious. When I say no," she continued, "she gives a deep sigh and says nothing. When I asked her if she wanted to see you, she shook her head and even said quite emphatically, 'Don't go round to Nopphon. Don't go disturbing his happiness under any circumstances.' But when people came to see her again, she asked about you again. I'm sure she badly wants to see you, but I don't know why she didn't want me to come round. I was rather doubtful, but in the end, I couldn't stand it any longer, so I slipped away and came round to see you. But I didn't tell her. I said the doctor had told me to go and buy medicine. But the doctor knew the truth about where I was going."

I could scarcely believe it. Why had Mom Ratchawong Kirati's condition deteriorated so suddenly? And why had she kept calling out my name when she was delirious? But everything her aunt said was true. When she had finished I did not ask any further questions. I was deeply shocked and concerned for Mom Ratchawong Kirati's life. We hurried straight round to her house. When we got near, I was urged not to let her know, under any circumstances, that anyone had called me. I gave my word.

I was led into the living room. A moment later the doctor looking after Mom Ratchawong Kirati came to have a word with me. He informed that the patient's condition was beyond hope. It was merely a matter of whether it was sooner or later. I also learned from the doctor that Mom Ratchawong Kirati's relatives had all expressed the opinion that there must be a special relation-ship between the two of us, and that for this reason, she ought to have a chance to see me before she died. I sat composed as I listened. Inside, my heart was filled with indescribable grief.

I waited for about ten minutes. Her aunt came out and told me that I had come at a good time, because Mom Ratchawong Kirati was conscious and her condition reasonably stable.

"Is Khunying ready for me to go and see her yet?" I asked.

"Please just wait another moment. She's getting dressed."

"Why does she have to get dressed?" I exclaimed in surprise. "Didn't you say she was very ill? Even the doctor said as much."

She sat down and explained. "She is very ill, that's right. And I don't know why she wants to get dressed. I protested and pointed out that it was Khun Nopphon, a close friend, who'd come to see her, and that there was no need to worry about getting dressed. She smiled—the first time I've really seen her smile since she fell ill— and brushed aside my objections. 'It really is most essential for me to dress up nicely to receive a dear friend. Suthan,' she said, turning to her younger sister. 'Please help me to get dressed. Dress me up really nicely, the way you know I like. Please do my hair again and put my lipstick on, the way I have it; and bring me some nice dresses from the wardrobe for me to choose from. Suthan, please help me to look beautiful again, just one more time before I die.' She smiled weakly, but both Suthan and I looked sad, and we could scarcely hold back our tears in our great sorrow. Eventually, we had to give in to her wishes. Suthan is getting her dressed now."

As she spoke, tears came to her eyes and I saw that she was trying to stifle a sob. The doctor lowered his head and listened quietly.

"She said to me, 'Have you told him I'm very ill and close to death?'" Mom Ratchawong Kirati's aunt continued. "I had to tell a lie for her sake, because I knew very well she didn't want you to know she was seriously ill. She was pleased and said, 'That's good. Please just tell Nopphon that I'm not very well. Don't alarm him.'"

When Mom Ratchawong Kirati's aunt had finished speaking, the three of us were silent. The living room was filled with a desolate air of gloom. After a while, she got up and went to see whether Mom Ratchawong Kirati was dressed yet. About ten minutes later, she came and told me that Mom Ratchawong Kirati was ready, and led me into the patient's room. As I walked towards the room, I felt a sense of sorrow and loneliness, as if I were visiting the corpse of someone I loved dearly, rather than a person who was still living.

Mom Ratchawong Kirati was lying down in the bedroom. As I entered the room, I was stunned for a moment. I had been expecting to find a sick person near to death, lying in a dark, stuffy room, full of bottles of medicine, with two or three people sitting there, weeping profusely. But I had pictured things quite different from reality. It was about five o'clock, and inside the room was bright with the late afternoon light which shone through each of the wide open windows. Mom Ratchawong Kirati was sitting on the bed, propped up by a pillow, with her legs stretched out along the length of the bed. A white blanket with a green Chinese-style pattern covered the lower part of her body. She wore a blouse of the same color, and on top of that, a black velvet jacket. This was to prevent me from seeing any part of her body which might lead me to the conclusion that she was on the verge of death. Her hair and face had been carefully done and concealed the extent of the deterioration in her condition. At just a glance, the red triangle shape of her lips almost deceived me into thinking that there was nothing wrong with her at all.

On a small bedside table stood a crystal vase containing a bunch of cheerful-looking fresh red christmas flowers. Two bird cages hung from the window with *kiribun* birds in them. The birds hopped about, chirping merrily. Everything in the room had been arranged tastefully. There was no sign that it was the room of someone who was terminally ill. I almost began to think I had been misled or something.

When she saw me standing there in the room, Mom Ratcha-wong Kirati put down the book she had been holding so as to show me she had been reading before I went in.

"Nopphon, please come and sit here," she said, indicating a chair by the bed. "I'm a little unwell, so I have to receive you in bed."

I was shocked when I heard her voice, because it was so hoarse and weak, I could scarcely hear her. I went and sat down quietly on the chair. "I was concerned about you, so I've come to see you."

"Thank you so much. I knew you hadn't forgotten me." She smiled cheerfully while turning her head in the direction of the woman standing keeping an eye on her at the head of the bed. "This is Suthan, my younger sister, who has found love and happiness in marriage, as I once told you."

I bowed in Suthan's direction.

"Everyone can go off and have a rest now, including you, Suthan," said Mom Ratchawong Kirati. "Leave me alone with Nopphon," she added.

The others exchanged glances. I remained silent.

"Please don't be concerned, because I'm not seriously ill."

Suthan went over and had a word with her aunt. A moment later, the doctor whispered to me not to talk with her for too long or make her tired. When everyone had left the room, Mom Ratchawong Kirati glanced in my direction with a look of contentment in her eyes. I pulled my chair up close to the bed.

"I didn't think I'd see you today. I didn't think I'd ever see you again, even for one last time in my life." She gazed at me, her eyes never flinching.

"I'm right here in front of you, now, and I'll stay as long as you want me," I replied solemnly.

"That's impossible, Nopphon, because you're not mine."

"I don't undertsand what you mean."

"That's right. You wouldn't understand, because you've never, ever understood, right from the first day we met." There seemed to be a mocking look in her eyes.

"Please tell me what else it is that I don't understand."

"You don't understand anything. Not a single thing. You don't even understand yourself."

I could not interpret her meaning. I looked at her uncertainly. She reached under another pillow and took out a sheet of paper. "This is a painting I did myself after returning from Japan. I'd like to give it to you as a wedding present."

I took the picture and looked at it with interest. It was a water-color depicting a stream flowing past the foot of a mountain, which was densely covered with trees. On the other side of the stream was a small path which passed over an overhanging rock, parts of which were tall, parts uneven with rocks of different sizes, and where creeping plants and wild flowers of different colors grew in a line along the rock. Further down, on a large rock, almost touching the water, sat two figures. The scene was depicted from a distance. In the bottom corner, written in small letters, was the word Mitake. I tried to fathom Mom Ratcha-wong Kirati's motive in giving me this small gift.

"It's not very good, Nopphon, but my heart and soul went into it, so it's a fitting wedding gift for you." When I looked up and met her eyes, she asked, "Do you remember, Nopphon, what happened there?"

I recalled the incident at Mount Mitake quite clearly, and I was beginning vaguely to understand what Mom Ratchawong Kirati meant.

"I fell in love there," I replied.

"We fell in love, Nopphon," she said, closing her eyes. "You fell in love there and your love died there. But for someone else, love still flourishes in a wasted body." Tears trickled down from beneath her closed eyelids. Mom Ratchawong Kirati sat silently in exhaustion. I looked at that body with love and grief.

A week later, Mom Ratchawong Kirati died. I was present during those last dark hours, together with all her friends and close relatives. Before the end, she asked for a pencil and paper. She wanted to say a last word to me, but her voice had gone, and all her strength. Thus it was, that on a piece of paper she wrote, "I die with no one to love me, yet content that I have someone to love."

* * * * *

THOSE KIND OF PEOPLE

Mom Luang Chomchailai emerged from the house carrying a foreign literary work and went over to the summer pavilion which stood in the garden, some distance away. She sat down by herself, opened the book, and began to read. It was after-noon and there was a pleasant breeze. The *taeo* tree in front of the pavilion had shed all of its leaves and was a mass of pink blossom. All around, it was quiet, except, that is, in the heart of this girl, as she sat there reading. She seemed unable to con-centrate on her book and kept looking up and gazing ahead, lost in thought, until the sound of a car engine broke her reverie. A large, ivory-colored vehicle pulled away from the house, with Chao Khun and Khunying Sisawat Boriban seated inside. Chomchailai put her book down and just sat there looking pensive.

Chomchailai was nearly twenty and at an age when most people can think only about love. But despite her background, her beauty, and her charm, she had had little chance for such thoughts. Seeing her parents sitting there in that smart car which had just left the house reminded her of the ever-present conflict that existed between her and them. Although it did not appear to be a very big issue, Chomchailai could not help feeling that it ran rather deep.

First published in *Sayam Samai*, March 1950

It had all started over her education. Chao Khun Sisawat was of the opinion that if you were a Thai, and you had not been to study in America or England, you were really a nobody. So he had advised his daughter to go and further her studies in America. He had even said that she did not have to study any-thing too demanding, and that if she went to America for two or three years, studied make-up, got some kind of diploma and came back speaking English, then that would be good enough. He had anticipated that a girl like Chomchailai would be excited at the mention of America, which had been getting a lot of good publicity—both from American films, and all the nice things in the shop—and seize upon his advice eagerly.

But Chao Khun Sisawat was astounded when his daughter refused on the grounds that she did not want to go and study in America, and that even if she had, it would not have been just for the sake of getting a piece of paper and learning to speak English. She wanted something more real. Chomchailai pointed out to her father that there had been hundreds of Thais who had gone to study in America and England, but that she could not see that there had been any change or improvement in the lives of the majority of people.

"What's this you're saying, Tiu?" (for that was her nickname) said Chao Khun Sisawat in surprise. "You mean you can't see just how much our country has changed and progressed? We have beautiful buildings and magnificent roads, we have bright lighting all over, and there are luxurious cars on on the roads. The progress is almost miraculous. When I was young, I never saw things like this."

An argument developed between father and daughter when Chomchailai asked who it was that enjoyed the fruits of this progress. In the end, Chao Khun Sisawat had to admit the truth in what his daughter was saying—that just beyond the outskirts of the city, there were no signs of any development, nor were there any bright lights. She told him that if the aim of studying abroad was merely to enable the educated and others of the same class to enjoy themselves in their own tiny group, then she did not want to go. Chao Khun tried to placate her. "You shouldn't go worrying too much about *those* kind of people," he said, referring to the people who lived outside Bangkok, the poor, and all those people who were not of the same class as Chao Khun himself. "They've always lived like that. They're used to it and they don't really need any more."

This kind of explanation made Chomchailai increasingly more certain that there was something very wrong about the kind of ideas her father had expressed. Why was it that people such as those in her circles enjoyed one way of life, while *those* kind of people had a completely different one? The only explanation there seemed to be was, "Oh, they've always lived like that. They're content with their lot." Chomchailai would secretly ask herself, half in doubt, half mockingly, "Who says they're content with their lot? Is it them? Or is it the people who want them to be content with their lot, who say it?"

Two weeks earlier, Chomchailai had gone to chat with the cook. She learned that one of the cook's children had been ill in bed for five or six days, so she asked the cook what she had done about treatment. "The child's got a tummy-ache and a bit of a temperature," the cook said. "I've bought some medicine for the stomach, and in a couple of days or so, it should have cleared up."

"But you can't be sure," said Chomchailai. "It might not be just a simple stomachache and fever. There's a typhoid epidemic at the moment. And if it's typhoid, that's really dangerous. You should get a doctor to come and see her, or else send her to the hospital.

You don't seem very concerned. Anyone would think you didn't care about your child."

The cook was shocked. "My goodness, what makes you think I don't love my child? It's just that there's no time to think about it because I'm tied down with housekeeping all day long. I don't know any doctor, anyway, and even if I did get one to come, I'd never be able to afford the cost of the medicine or his fees."

The little girl who was ill, was seven. She lay there with her eyes open listening to the adults without understanding what they were talking about. She did not realize how seriously ill she was, and thought she would soon be fully recovered as her mother had said, as she gently comforted the child. She had no doubts about her mother's love and thought that her mother was one of the cleverest people in the world. Chomchailai went and knelt down beside the child who lay on a mat in the rather un-tidy and stuffy room. Her lips were dry and her eyes looked drowsy. She was very hot. Chomchailai asked how she was and then told the cook that she was going to send the child to hospital quickly. Then off she went, to see her mother, Khun-ying, to tell her that the cook's child had been lying sick for five or six days without any visit from a doctor. She suspected it was typhoid, so she was going to arrange for the child to be sent to hospital, and so wondered if she could use the driver to take her by car.

"Tiu," cried the shocked Khunying, "you're forgetting yourself just a little bit too much. You want to ferry Yai Khram's scruffy little child in our car?" Well, I'm afraid I just can't allow it. And your father wouldn't be very pleased, either."

Chomchailai pointed out that the circumstances were unusual and that it was a case of getting a sick child to hospital. But Khunying Sisawat would not listen. "That's all very well," she said, "but I just don't see that there's any need. In the old days when people were sick and had to go to hospital, they didn't go by car, did they? So how was it they managed? Tiu, don't go getting involved with them too much. They'll only start forget-ting themselves. And as for this illness business, they're used to it, and they have their own methods of treatment. After all, if they hadn't, they'd all be dead by now. Just look at the people upcountry. They've never ever seen a doctor or a hospital, so how is it they manage to survive, generation after generation? And people like Yai Khram are a hundred times luckier than those kind of people, because they've come to live in Bangkok, among people like us. They get more than enough medicine and up-to-date advice for people of their class, and they certainly don't need any more. So, Tiu, you shouldn't go interfering and getting worked up about those kind of people."

Chomchailai remained silent and quietly took leave of her mother. Her mother thought that Chomchailai had been convinced by her reasoning, but in fact her daughter was feeling somewhat distressed. She was used to hearing people talk about "*those* kind of people," saying, "they don't need anything more, they're content with their lot," and "they've been living their own way for donkeys' years." She had heard it from her father, from her mother and from all her relatives. But she knew perfectly well that it was not true that "*those* kind of people" did not need anything more. She was fully aware that the cook loved and cared for her youngest child as much as her own mother did for her, or any mother of her class would for her child, and that the cook wanted her child to receive proper medical care from a doctor or the hospital. But it was just that she had to work too hard and she received too little money to be able to give her child good treatment.

Chomchailai's mother's words, which showed that she believed that the fruits of progress were the monopoly of her own class, that "*those* kind of people" had no rights and that they should not

dare to talk about or ask for a share in them, made Chom-chailai
wonder where such an idea had originally come from, and how it
had continued to survive. That day she quietly arranged for the
gardener to help take the cook's child to hospital by *samlo*. While
the child was in hospital, Chomchailai went to visit her twice. The
poor little girl lay sick there for about ten days and then died. She
had typhoid.

The cook was grief-stricken. She cried at the loss of the daughter she loved, and lamented that she had accumulated insufficient
merit. It never occurred to her that she had lost her daughter
because of poverty. It was nobody's fault and nobody could
do anything about it, just as it had been when her husband had
deserted her. She had been taught that what happened in life rested
entirely upon fate and Heaven and Earth. Chomchailai suspected
that if that little girl had been her younger sister and her mother
had been concerned and sent her to hospital right at the beginning,
then the child might not have died. Perhaps Heaven and Earth
would not have demanded that little girl's life.

These events made a deep impression on Chomchailai and she
could not help brooding over them. Chao Khun and Khunying
Sisawat just could not understand that their attitude to life and that
of their daughter, were worlds apart. They both tried to persuade,
and sometimes even forced, Chomchailai to mingle as much as
possible among people of her own class, with a view to finding
a suitable future partner. Chomchailai understood perfectly well
what her parents had in mind, but at the same time, she felt that her
tastes were very different from the young men in those circles. She
could not understand why they frittered away their lives, nor their
idea that people who did so little work and had such an easy life,

should have the right to an overwhelm-ing abundance of happiness to which their own lives gave proof.

Chomchailai's spirits lifted when she met Bao, the son of their driver, Chun. Bao was nineteen and lived with his father at her house. He had had his elementary schooling at a nearby temple school and had then gone on to a private school. After finishing sixth grade, he had gone on to study about construction at a vocational school and would finish his course the following year. Chomchailai enjoyed seeing Bao, because she felt there was more to him than the other young men in her own social circles. She noticed that his knowledge and ideas went far beyond what might be expected from someone who had had such a patchy education as his. Bao told her that he usually spent his holidays reading books in a public library, and since he was a member of that library, he would borrow books to take home and read at night. When he was at the private school, his father had told him to pay attention to his studies, because he, himself, had not done so sufficiently when he was young, and he had ended up as a driver. Bao heeded his father's advice and had set his mind to his studies and read widely as he grew older. He knew that being a driver, or doing other jobs where you used physical strength, were not lowly occupations, and people who were employed in jobs that demanded physical labor, were not necessarily unable to improve their position, or without the chance of gaining the admiration and respect of the people. He had learned from books that the majority of people in Europe and America worked in factories, and he was proud of the fact that his father was a driver, a job which required some knowledge of engines and machines. He knew that workers in foreign countries had the opportunity to work their way up to a higher position by using their free time to study at evening institutes or at night classes, or alternatively, they could seek knowledge from libraries. The people who occupied the top positions in foreign governments, right up to the level of prime minister, included many who, like his father, were from the working classes. Thus he did not feel in the least bit discouraged that his father did not have the money to send him to university, even though it put him at a disadvantage com-pared with those of his own age who were fortunate enough to go. "But knowledge all comes from books," Bao would say con-fidently. "If we really want it, it can't escape us. But if we don't really want it, then we won't get it, that's for sure, even if we do go and study at university."

Chomchailai thought that she and Bao could have become good friends, if only he were from the same class as her. But since he was not, it was almost as if there were a barrier between them, and that the most she could do was to talk with him across this barrier. She could get no closer to him than this, and even this would draw disapproving looks from her parents. How had this barrier come about? Who had set it up? And was it right, or of any use to the people, if it continued to exist? Chomchailai thought that without such a barrier they would have got on well together.

Just as Chomchailai picked up her book again and began to read, she noticed someone coming over towards her, carrying a large case. "Goodness, it's you, Bao," she called out in greeting, as the man drew near. "You're all dressed up like a civil servant from the city, off somewhere on an inspection tour." In fact Bao did indeed look as if he was going on a long journey. He stood outside the pavilion, waiting until Chomchailai invited him in, and then sat down in a chair opposite her. As he sat there, Chom-chailai noticed the serious look in his eyes. She realized that there must be some special significance in him coming to see her dressed like that and carrying a large case.

"Where are you going, Bao?"

"I thought I'd come and say goodbye," he said with difficulty.

"Are you going upcountry or on holiday somewhere?"

"No, not at all. I . . . I just want to leave this house. I'm mov-ing away."

Chomchailai sat there in shocked silence. She wondered what had made him decide to leave the house. And at the same time, she felt that if he left, it would mean losing a friend whom she thought she got on better with than most other people.

"I didn't want to tell you," he said, his head bowed. When he looked up again, he was more composed. "My father said that Chao Khun isn't very happy about my continued residence in this house," he said. "My crime is that I'm from a different class to his daughter, and he thinks it's sinful for his daughter to talk with the likes of me."

"I know what my father thinks," Chomchailai said quietly. "It's something I totally disagree with. Ever since I was old enough to think, he referred to you as '*those* kind of people'; and between his world and '*those* kind of people,' there stands a huge barrier. But I think that one day that barrier will disappear and the two groups will be able to mix freely and become one and the same group."

"The barrier won't just disappear like that," Bao said solemnly. "Not until '*those* kind of people' destroy it and we all work together to build bridges, roads, houses, hospitals, and schools which we can *all* use."

"And not just people like my father," Chomchailai added. "I'm really ever so sorry, Bao, that you have to leave because of what my father thinks, which is something I utterly disagree with anyway."

"But I'm not a bit sorry," said Bao. "Your words have given me greater strength to study, so that one day I might be able to prove whether you are right or not." Bao rose and said goodbye to Chomchailai with a respectful *wai*.

"What do you want to be in the future, Bao?" she asked.

"If I can, I want to be an engineer," he replied gently, but with a hint of seriousness in his voice. "I want to build whatever I can. But of course, before we can build, we may first have to tear down some things, or perhaps even many things. Otherwise it might be impossible to build."

Chomchailai watched him go. He was a well-proportioned young man and walked with a firm and resolute step. He reminded her of a warrior on the battlefield. The thought flashed through her mind that one day she might choose a warrior from "*those* kind of people" to be her partner in life. She wanted to share in the task of tearing down that massive barrier.

LEND US A HAND

Lend us a hand.

When someone says this, someone else responds.

"Lend us a hand."

"Right."

And then hands, shoulders, and backs turn up and the various tasks are completed. It is what they say here, what they say there, what they have been saying for donkeys' years, and what they are still saying today. They are common, everyday words you hear everywhere. People are so used to hearing them that no one takes any notice and no one thinks they mean anything.

And then one day, doubts began to arise as to whether these words, which people had long heard and spoken, really did have no meaning. And eventually people began to have discussions among themselves to find out the meaning. Such doubts and investigations that I refer to, did not occur among members of the Royal Institute or committees of experts. Instead they developed from the discussions of poor people, a group whose doubts were a result of real events in their own lives.

First published in *Piyamit*, October 1950

Inside a hut, whose roof and four walls were covered with nipa palm leaves, the middle-aged owner lay sick on an old mat. His face was drawn and pale and his body thin. But the broadness of his shoulders indicated that before his illness, his physical strength was his source of livelihood, with some left over to be of service to others, too. Although he had used it for the benefit of others, now, he had become a burden to other people.

Slowly, the man propped himself up and sat unsteadily, spooning up the plain rice gruel that his wife had prepared for him. He sipped two or three spoonfuls and then shook his head. His wife comforted him and begged him to force himself to eat just a little bit more. He forced himself to take another five or six spoonfuls and then stopped. "This time, I don't think Mo In's herbal medicine on its own is going to be effective," he said to his wife. "I can feel myself getting weaker every day. Old Khian came to see me this morning and he told me that the modern doctor at the shop at the top of the street had said that to cure me, I'd need several injections. I'd like to try it, to keep me alive, but we haven't got the money. I'd like you to go and see the owner of the green brick house near the end of the lane and try to borrow 100 baht from him."

"What, with us being so poor, is he going to trust us?" his wife said pessimistically.

"He asked me to lend him a hand round at his house two or three times," the sick man said, citing his good deeds from the past. "He's bound to feel some compassion for me. We're going through a hard time now. Try having a word with him in case we might be in luck."

In case we might be in luck . . .

The words struck Pui, his wife, raising her hopes. That evening, at about eight o'clock, she braved the dark and went to the green brick house which was about two kilometers down the *soi*. When she got there, she found the main gate, at the front of the house, firmly bolted. For some time she stood there, craning her neck against the high, barbed wire fence. She did not dare to call out. Then a light from a torch inside shone on Pui. There was the sound of footsteps hurrying and then someone stopping by the fence. "What do you think you're hanging around here for?" a voice demanded sharply.

The voice made Pui's heart tremble. "My name's Pui. My husband's name is Maen. We live in a hut in the middle of the rice field up near the entrance to the *soi*. I've come to see the owner."

"He doesn't see strangers at this time of night," the woman's voice replied from the other side.

"My husband, Maen, has worked at the house several times."

"These days you can't trust people. There're robberies nearly every day. He doesn't open the gate to just anyone from outside."

"My husband is very ill . . ."

"These days people use all kinds of tricks," came the voice from the other side. "If you have something to see him about, wait till tomorrow. Don't come sneaking round here at night. It could be dangerous for you."

The woman was right. These days it was difficult to trust people. People did use all kinds of tricks, Pui reflected as she braved her way home through the dark for another two kilometers.

In case we might be in luck . . .

The next morning Pui left the house and returned to the green brick house. This time she got through the main gate with no difficulty, and went and sat politely on the floor, just in front of the living room door, waiting for the owner. A while later, the owner of the house, a plump and robust-looking man, entered the room. The moment he glanced at the pathetic figure who had come to see him, a feeling of annoyance registered on his face. He sat down on the padded sofa and nodded in Pui's direction. Pui told him who she was and where she was from. "My husband's been ill for many days. Neither he nor I know who to turn to for the doctor's fees," she continued. "So he asked me to come and see you and ask to borrow 100 baht. Once he's better and can work again, we'll save the money he earns and return it to you later."

The owner pulled a face, as if he had been made to chew on the bitter *borapet* plant. Nevertheless, he did not beat about the bush in his reply. "A hundred baht is no trifling amount, you know. I don't know anything about Maen. Just giving it away like that isn't the way things are done."

"My husband said that you asked him to lend a hand round at your house, two or three times, and that in a time of hardship, you would surely be kind and help," Pui continued to plead.

"It's difficult. Difficult," the owner said, gesturing with his hand. "It's true, I have called upon Nai Maen's labor. But you can't compare labor with money. Labor is something everyone has. It's something you can find very easily, and as much of it as you want. It's something you only have to ask for, wouldn't you say? But money—that's another matter. That's not so easy to find. It's something people keep to themselves. You ought to know that it's something that's difficult to talk about."

"Yes sir, I do. It is difficult to talk about," Pui said, forcing herself to repeat the owner's words. But she did not give up. "But my husband is very ill. I'm really at my wits' end. I don't know who else to turn to."

"I sympathize with you." The owner began to get up from his chair to show that the conversation with Pui, which was not productive for him in any way whatsoever, was over. "I think that in a case of hardship such as this, you should get in touch with your

MP. It's not my responsibility." He got up. "I'll tell you what," he added. "Wait a minute . . ." He disappeared inside for a moment and then returned with a bottle of medi-cine in his hands. "Since Nai Maen came to help me, I'd like to offer him this bottle of medicine to try for his fever." He gave the bottle to Pui and said finally, "Perhaps he'll be in luck . . ."

The next day, the news that Pui had gone to the owner of the green brick house for help and had been humiliatingly turned away, spread among Nai Maen's neighbors. That the owner had refused to give help, was his business; but the fact that he had spoken in a derogatory fashion about the labor of comrades who had made sacrifices without expecting anything in return, fired their determination and increased their solidarity. Thus, Nai Maen's neighbors arranged a collection among themselves, and when they had sufficient money to call the modern doctor from the shop at the entrance to the *soi* to come and treat their comrade, they took the money and handed it over to Pui. From the moment the patient received proper medical treatment from the modern doctor, his fortunes changed. He began to recover from the serious illness. His strength began to return to normal and his condition steadily improved until he was almost back to normal.

One day, three or four of Nai Maen's friends gathered to talk in his hut, and he, too, sat listening to the conversation of his comrades. That day they discussed the question of their labor. Were they true, those insulting words the owner of the green house had said, about their labor being insignificant and not worthy of praise? Nai Maen's comrades admitted that there was something in what the owner had said when he spoke contemp-tuously of their labor as being insignificant. "You can't compare it with his money," one comrade explained. "They're worlds apart. Us lot already know that money's like a magic crystal. Anyone with money can create anything. But us lot, with just our labor, can scarcely manage to fill our stomachs from one day to the next."

"And those who are rich and have lots of money," asked one of the comrades, "what did they do to get so rich?"

"The rich invest their money in trade and the money just comes pouring in on its own."

"Where do they get the money to invest from?"

"How do I know?"

"That's strange, you know," Nai Maen broke in. "I'd like to know where it came from in the first place."

The group were silent for a moment. Then a third comrade spoke. "I still wonder just how much harder than us people who are rich have to work for the money to come pouring in and pil-ing up to the point of overflowing. And as for us, why do we have to remain as impoverished as this?"

"The rich don't work any harder than us at all," the first of the comrades explained. "In fact it's us who have to work, almost to the breaking point. But as we all know, friends, it's money that creates everything, money that builds each and every thing. You can't go comparing yourself with them."

"My three comrades," Nai Maen said, gesturing as he spoke. "I'd say it's not money at all, friends, which creates everything and which builds each and every thing." The three comrades turned and stared at him simultaneously, each waiting with interest for what he would say. "Who is it," Nai Maen continued slowly and solemnly, "who goes into the forests and fells the trees with their sturdy arms? Who is it, who floats the logs down-river, night and day exposed to the rain and sun, before they reach their destination? Who is it, who sits with their back bent double, dragging their arms back and forth, all day long, sawing the wood into planks ready for building houses? And who is it who cries 'heave-ho' and joins hands on the pile-driver, as the foundation pile is driven deep into the earth, and sweat streams down their bodies like the water from a fountain, as a large con-crete building takes shape? And who is it," Nai Maen said, turn-ing to one comrade, who was a carpenter, "who builds the houses and even the magnificent royal palaces? Isn't it poor people like you? Is it money which creates everything, or is it, in fact, simply our strength, our skill and our sweat?"

The three comrades nodded slowly in agreement. Bewildered agreement. And then Nai Maen continued. "Who is it, who wades through the water with his faithful buffalo, breaking up the ground under the scorching sun before transplanting the rice seedlings? Before long, golden ears will burst forth all over the fields to provide for Thais all over the country, with enough left over to sell abroad in exchange for beautiful, attractive goods which are presented to the rich and well-to-do for their extra-vagant use." Nai Maen turned to the second comrade, who was a farmer. "And who the hell is it, that grows the rice to support the whole country? Who the hell is it, who prevents us from starving? It's your poor farmers again. And where does this idea, that money creates everything, come from, and that the rich landowners are our protectors?"

The comrades all remained silent. Their eyes shone, and they stared at Nai Maen's face as he continued. "And who is it, who breaks up the ground with his spade and digs out the lumps of soil to make canals, full of water, for everyone to use for bathing, drinking, or traveling by boat? Who is it, who carries the soil and levels it to make roads for people to travel along, and for the rich and well-to-do to drive their cars along for pleasure?" Nai Maen turned to the third comrade, who was a laborer. "Who is it, who builds the roads and canals? Why, it's the likes of you, isn't it, who builds them?"

Nai Maen gave a loud and terrifying laugh. "Who the hell is it," he added, "who builds everything? Is it money, or is it damn well labor that does the job? Before, I never thought about this, not until I heard the contemptuous words of the owner of that green brick house. Then I began to look at things, and I saw the reality that I have just told you."

The discussion between the four villagers continued for a long time. It was the first time they had talked seriously about something. They were not merely moaning or grumbling to pass the time of day, with the same feeling of pessimism as before. They were beginning to think that in the search for truth, you did not have to rely on the teachings of scholars of the Royal Institute. Real life, which they encountered every day, provided them with a more valuable lesson, if they awoke from their deep sleep and used their own observations to properly analyze things.

In the solitude of a pitch-dark, moonless night, the rain, which had been falling heavily since dusk, continued to pour down. People in the houses in the *soi* were all sound asleep. It was odd that a car should emerge from a *soi* and head out towards the main road, along a street that was flooded by the rain. The car drove out slowly, rocking from side to side. The driver was clearly trying to avoid the puddles and potholes that existed in places. But eventually, he drove the car down into a pothole that had been concealed by the flood water. He changed gear and revved the engine. But the right-hand wheel, which had sunk into the pothole, merely spun round and round, splattering water out in all directions, and the car did not budge an inch forwards. He revved the engine again. He made a second and third attempt, but to no avail, for the wheel was spinning round on the spot and merely digging itself even deeper into the ground than before.

Although the air was cool, the driver's face was covered with beads of sweat. It was not simply the effort of driving; it was fear, which was discernible in his bulging eyes and pale face. His hands dropped from the steering wheel. With a deep sigh of despair, he cried, "Lord Buddha, how cruel you are." It was none other than the owner of the green brick house.

The sound of a woman's voice, weak and trembling, emerged from the back of the car. "You've never done any good deeds at all, so what God is going to show any pity?"

"What do you mean, 'never'?" he objected, as if he wanted God to hear. "Last month I sent 1,000 baht to make merit on the monk's birthday."

"But you pointed out to me, that making a donation was as good as investing money in your business," the voice from inside said. "You said, give them a thousand and you'd get it back in tens and hundreds of thousands. Will God accept this kind of merit-making?"

The owner of the green brick house gave a deep sigh and was silent for a while. The woman who had spoken out from the back of the car was his wife. She was suffering from cholera and needed medical treatment urgently. By chance, there were no other men at home at all that night. Their eldest son had gone off to Bang-saen with his younger brothers, taking the driver and his father's large car. So the owner of the house had to take his wife through the darkness in the small car, in order to get her to a doctor quickly.

Just then, he looked behind him and saw his wife leaning over, her head resting on the maid's shoulder and her eyes closed with exhaustion. By the dim light inside the car, the pale, sweat-drenched face of the man who worshipped money as a god, was visible. In a time of trouble like this, when the god of money could not help, he called upon the god of mercy for help, whom, all the time he had held an advantage over other men, he had never worshipped, nor ever even given any thought to.

"I'm at my wits' end, Mani," he confided in the maid. "There's no way we can get the car out of the pothole, unless we get two or three people to help push it. But there's no one at all at home."

There was a flash of lightning. For an instant it lit up the roofs on a row of huts in the middle of the fields. Then came the roar of thunder. The sick woman shrieked with fear and alarm. The owner of the house leaned over and touched his wife on the shoulder, not knowing what words of comfort to offer. "Is God angry with us?" she murmured.

When the lightning had momentarily illuminated the fields, Mani had been looking out of the partly open side window. Her eyes lit up with hope. "It looks as if Nai Maen's house is around here," she said, as the crack of thunder faded. "Shall I go and get Nai Maen and ask him to help push the car?"

"Oh, Nai Maen," the owner of the house cried, almost startling the sick woman. "The Nai Maen I used to ask to give me a hand at home? Go on, hurry off to his hut. He'll help to get our car out of the hole for sure. Go on, hurry. There's no time to be lost."

The maid carefully leaned her mistress up against the inside corner of the car and then picked up a torch and walked across the fields, in the fine rain, towards the hut, which appeared as a faint shadow in front of her.

A while later, a torch light appeared along the dike, directly in front of the car, and gradually came nearer. The owner of the house saw the muscular figure of a man walking along the dike. He mopped the sweat from his face with a handkerchief. He stared over towards the fields and then turned anxiously to his wife who was slumped over.

As Nai Maen and the maid crossed the ditch next to the road and approached the car, the owner quickly opened the door and leaned out, ready to greet Nai Maen. The wind blew rain into his face and body. Under normal circumstances he would have found it difficult to tolerate such annoyances.

"Nai Maen? My dear fellow," the owner greeted him loudly, almost shouting. Nai Maen stopped a couple of yards short of the open car door. He was wearing a sarong with a cloth tied round his head. His face and dark, muscular body glistened in the rain. Nai Maen's face was solemn. "I need help," the owner continued breathlessly. "My car's stuck. I've tried, but I can't get it out. I need someone to help push to get it out. Give me a bit of a hand and help push, will you, there's a good fellow?"

Nai Maen stared straight into the rich man's face. "You and I don't know each other," he said emphatically. "I don't go giving away my labor just like that. That's not the way things are done."

The owner of the house was shocked. But he pulled himself together and continued. "Whatever fee you ask, I'll be only too pleased to give you."

"Human labor doesn't have any value, though, does it?" Nai Maen said harshly. "It's something you can find easily. It's in plentiful supply. So please, go and look somewhere else," he said, turning away as if to go back.

The rich man's eyes became wild. "Don't go, Nai Maen," he screamed, almost at the top of his voice. "My wife is seriously ill. I'm taking her to the doctor's. If I delay, it could be critical. Please help me. I'm at my wits' end."

Nai Maen turned and faced the owner of the green brick house, who had got out of the car and was following him. "Labor is worthless," he said. "It's money that's important. You try using your money to push it. Maybe that'll help get your car out of the hole." And having said that, Nai Maen walked rapidly back to the dike, without a glance behind. The owner of the house hurried after him and as Nai Maen stepped up on to the dike, he grabbed him round the waist, pleading for help. Nai Maen pushed his hands away, and the rich man lost his footing and toppled over into the flooded field. As Nai Maen was about to continue on his way, he heard a woman's trembling voice behind.

"Please have pity on a very sick woman. Lord have mercy on this life." Nai Maen stood rooted to the spot. The plaintive sound of her voice so tore at his heart, he was almost over-whelmed. He dug in his heels and gritted his teeth to maintain his composure. Then he turned and spoke directly to the owner of the house, who was struggling to his feet. "I'm not as hard-hearted as you. Wait here a moment and then I'll be out to help." He went off rapidly along the dike. The rich man stood panting against the car in the middle of the rain, staring into the pitch-dark fields. He saw a dim light appear in the hut. He saw people going back and forth. He scarcely took his eye off the hut for a single moment. His eyes were full of hope, as if that hut was the abode of God. After a while, he saw indistinct shadows approaching along the dike. Nai Maen was returning with two companions. He was carrying a crowbar and walking ahead of his companions, who were carrying three or four planks. The rich man gazed at the three men as if he were looking at his God. Nai Maen's face was as stern as before. He did not say a word.

He set to work immediately. With his strong arms, he used the crowbar to loosen the soil around the sunken wheel, and then raise it. His two companions inserted the planks against the wheel. When they had done this, Nai Maen raised his right arm to wipe away the mixture of sweat and rain from his face. He threw the crowbar down on the ground and turning to the rich man, who was standing quietly behind, he ordered him to get back in the car and start up, while the three of them gave him a push.

The owner of the house jumped into the driver's seat in a hurry, started up and put the car in gear. Nai Maen bent down and pushed with all his might against the mudguard of the wheel that was stuck. His two companions pushed with all their strength from behind. The engine roared, and where before, it had been unable to drag the car out, now, in a moment, the vehicle had leaped out of the concealed hole.

The rich man stopped the car. He opened the door and beaming, he shouted to Nai Maen, "Thank you, my dear fellow. If my wife gets to the doctor in time and survives, it really is because of you and your friends."

"But when I was critically ill and close to death, and I survived, it wasn't thanks to your help," Nai Maen retorted.

"We only talk of the Lord Buddha," the sick woman mumured. "But we're not close to him in the way you poor people are."

The engine roared, and the car carrying the sick woman drove straight out through the drizzle to the main road. Nai Maen picked up the crowbar and put it over his shoulder and with his two companions, he headed back to his hut in the pitch-black fields.

THE AWAKENING

The row of huts stood on a patch of slimy, muddy ground. A large, smart saloon car pulled up in front. The gentleman who owned the vehicle had some business to attend to in the little *soi* at the side of the row of huts, but since his vehicle was a little too big to go down the *soi*, he had parked it there and got out and walked, leaving his pretty wife alone in the car. After about ten minutes, he returned to find his wife sitting slumped over in the car, breathing softly and with a bottle of ammonia in her hand. His face paled in alarm at the thought that his wife had been mugged.

"If you'd been too long, I would have been completely unconscious in the car," the lady moaned.

"Which way did they go?" he asked immediately, at the same time patting the back pocket of his trousers, as if checking a weapon.

"Who?" his wife asked, also beginning to look anxious.

"The swines who mugged you."

The lady gradually recovered as she began to see the funny side. "Whatever made you think that? No one's mugged me."

"Oh. So what's the matter, then?"

First published in *Piyamit*, October 1952

"It's the smell of all that slime under those filthy huts. Get in quickly. It's making me dizzy. I don't know how these people can live here."

In a moment, the large, smart saloon car was gone.

How can these people live here? That is what everyone says. But few people ask why it is they have to come and live like this. Is it they themselves, or what, or who, that makes them have to live this way?

Am and Nim, a young married couple, have been living in a dirty hut over a slimy swamp for eight years now, since war-time, without ever using or even knowing about ammonia. They are so used to the smell of the slime, which they have had to inhale for the last eight years, that they scarcely notice any difference from the smell of clean water in the canals and dykes. They are so used to it that it is a part of their lives.

In front of their hut, and all along the front of the others, there is slimy mud. It has been like this every rainy season for many years and they are used to it. It is part of their lives. Inside the cramped and tumble-down hut are five people, a *samlo*, bedding, and the bare necessities of clothing piled up against the walls, with two wooden crates for putting all the odds and ends and property essential to the lives of those people. It looks as if they are all migrants, moving on from one place to the next, and this, merely a temporary refuge. Looked at this way, Am had been traveling and stopping off for twelve years, and he never dreams that his life of traveling might end before he dies.

When all the members of the family are together at daybreak and dusk, and with the *samlo* taking up a quarter of the space, it is rather cramped inside, resembling rather a temporary refuge from danger than a permanent residence. In fact, the day-to-day life of

Am and his family is like a flight from danger. Every day he has to face danger, simply in order to survive from one day to the next. Frequently he is disheartened at the thought of where the day's food is going to come from and what he is going to do about little Tum, his youngest, who has been lying feverish for three days, and where the money is going to come from to buy old woolen blankets for the two children when the cold season comes this year. These are minor threats; from time to time there are even greater ones which affect his life.

On one occasion, a typhoon struck Bangkok. People called it "Typhoon Songkran." The roar of the hurricane was terrifying as it howled through the trees and leaves. Dust and rubbish from the streets were blown into their room, as if it had been poured in there by a machine. The room shook as if it were being rocked by an earthquake. The two children ran and clung to their mother and grandmother in fright, while the two women rushed to close the doors and gather up their worthless possessions. Mother and children went and sat huddled in a corner of the hut, but Grandmother meanwhile lit a candle and prayed that the gods and Heaven and Earth would protect them. There was a crack of thunder over the roof and everyone shrieked and closed their eyes. When they opened them again, they all saw light from above pouring down into the room. Grandmother was overjoyed, thinking it was some miraculous power from on high, revealing its might before their very eyes. When they looked up, however, they realized the storm had blown some of the tiles off the roof, leaving a large, gaping hole.

Yes, it is the landlord's duty to see to repairs. But in times when everyone is looking for a home to rest their heads, and when rented huts the size of a garage or a stable are extremely difficult to find, proper regulations get temporarily shelved. Thus the landlord's reaction was that if they wanted to stay there, they could repair it themselves, and if they did not like it, they could find somewhere else. Though it was difficult for Am and Nim to see anything to like about it, moving would have been a hundred times more difficult. So Am just had to put up with the burden of repairing it himself. He had to take a day off work and run around borrowing money from a friend to buy the materials for the repairs, and then carry them out himself. To some of you, this may seem a trifling matter; but for him, earning only enough to live on from one day to the next, and with a family of five to support, it was a considerable burden.

Another major threat loomed. While he was helping a neighbor to carry some things, someone carelessly threw a jerry can so that it struck his foot. The corner of the can cut his foot, opening up a small wound. If he or his friends had known the correct way of treating it, it would have remained just a small wound that would have healed within two or three days. But because he did not know, it took a long time, and he had to endure even more pain than that caused by a bullet wound. In the beginning, he put a kind of beeswax on it, which was used for treating various conditions ranging from insect stings to cholera. He applied it to the wound and then went out on his *samlo* as usual. After that, the wound festered and the infection spread, so he covered it with a dressing on the advice of a neigh-bor and remained at home. For a fortnight he was unable to go out to work, until a kind gentleman in the street learned of this and gave him some sulphur ointment. The wound gradually healed until he was able to drive the *samlo* again, as before. How his family had to struggle to survive from day to day when he was unable to go out to work filled one with pity. It was like when you catch a fish, you put it down on the ground, and it struggles to the very last ounce of its strength to find a way, any way it can, back to the water. That was how much they struggled. "Struggle until the scales dry up," Am used to say to his friends.

As he limped around, worrying about how he was going to repay the debts he had accumulated while he had been off work, an evil thought flashed through his mind. He saw the image of an individual in army uniform, lying in wait and holding people up in lonely spots. It was one quick way of paying off his debts. He could not see any other. But a moment later, the long life of honesty he had lived in the past appeared shining brightly before him. He shook his head decisively two or three times, and the image of the fearsome man with a ruthless expression on his face and weapon in his hand, standing hidden in a dark and lonely spot, disappeared, never to return. "*Sathu*," he cried, raising his hands above his head. On the first day that he was able to walk properly, he pulled his vehicle out of the garage, or rather his bedroom. When he placed his feet on the pedals and leaned forward, putting his full weight on the soles of his feet, he felt a tingling sensation all over. "Oh, these old legs of mine, they're my life," he reflected with delight, as if the thought had never occurred to him before. "And these old hands of mine, right here on these handlebars of steel. These old hands of mine, callused and hard, they're my life, the foundation on which my life and wife's and children's are built . . . these old things, right here."

That afternoon, his son and daughter, who were between five and seven years old, were running in and out of the hut. Sometimes they would stand on the patio, in front of the door, and shielding their eyes, peer up the street in the direction their father came when he returned from work. Grandmother came out and picked morning glory from the ditch opposite, despite the glare of the sun. Mother was busy with something in the kitchen, and the two children could be heard grumbling and wondering when their father would be back. Then they would take their scruffy little selves back into the kitchen, only to be shooed away again because of their incessant stream of questions, which their mother could not answer. Then they would run back out to the front of the house and stare out in the same direction, grumbling and confiding in each other until they got fed up and went back inside.

The familiar sound of a bell rang out in front of their home, and the two children raced out, almost falling over and getting themselves covered in mud at the front of the hut. Once Am was standing on the patio at the front, the two children surrounded him, begging for sweets and asking all sorts of questions. He gave them a small packet of sweets, and with a sooty cloth, wiped the sweat that was running down his face and hands like drops of rain. He walked straight into the kitchen without answering the children's questions, and they forgot for a moment what they had been asking, as they were engrossed in sharing out the sweets.

"Why are you late?" Nim greeted him. "The children have been waiting and grumbling a lot. They were worried they wouldn't be going to Sanam Luang."

That afternoon, there was to be an official presentation of military weapons which America had sent to the Thai govern-ment. They had made announcemnts inviting the people to go and view the new weapons, and it had also been announced that there would be monks blessing the weapons of destruction so that they might be successsful and victorious. When the children heard the news they had begged their father to take them. As he had not taken them anywhere for several months, he gave in to their pleas and agreed to take them in the afternoon. And so it was, that they had been waiting eagerly for their father since before mid-day.

"Have you had lunch, yet?" his wife asked.

"Not yet. I'm absolutely starving." He went over to the rice pot, scooped some rice out onto a heavily scratched tin plate and then sat down in the middle of the room while his wife went to the pantry. She took out a dish of *nam phrik* which was left over from breakfast, and some salted fish, of which only the heads remained. When Grandmother came in with some fresh morning glory, he rubbed his hands with delight.

As he ate, Am told Nim why he was late home. He told her that just before mid-day, he had parked his *samlo* in the shade, near Khlong Lot. There were dozens of *samlo* drivers from the Northeast taking a break there. They were talking together in groups about the famine which their brothers in the Northeast were suffering and which they themselves were all too familiar with. One of them suggested that each of them ought to make a small contribution and their collection be sent to a newspaper, which would arrange for it to be distributed to their fellow northeasterners up there. Someone interrupted. "We bloody well don't have enough to live on from one day to the next," he said. "So how are you going to go helping others. If you're not careful, you'll end up a communist." Someone else supported him. "How much blood can you get out of a crab?" he demanded. "It's better to let the rich help them. We shouldn't go getting involved. It'll get political and there'll be a right bloody mess."

At that moment a fourth young man exploded. "What the hell's it got to do with politics?" he demanded. "It's about helping our starving brothers. But if that's what you're going to call politics, then I'm all for it! A right bloody mess, I call it, if we don't help. All we're talking about is helping—why should that get us into a bloody mess? And if that's what you call a bloody mess, then a bloody mess is all right by me. And when you say, 'wait and let the rich people help our brothers,' have you ever seen them even once stretch out a hand to help us? Just take us, working here in Bangkok. Have you ever seen your rich and your well-to-do give us any help? All they do is drive us away, don't they? When we were still living with our parents and our grandparents, working in the rice fields, the rich made money and rice available for us to borrow. Did they ever help us? When you fell upon hard times, when you had no rice to eat or grow, and they gave you rice, did they do it because they loved you? And when you had rice, how much of it did they take away? How many times their original loan was it? Don't you see? And you've still got the nerve to say, "wait for the rich to help us'! We sweat and toil away in the scorching sun, wading through mud in the paddy fields, exhausted almost to the point of dropping. The rice ripens, and then, do you know where it disappears to, and where all the money goes, and why we have to live on the breadline? I'm not clever enough to tell you how it disappears, but one thing I do know for sure is that our rice or our fruit can't just disappear into thin air. And I'd say it flows into the hands of those people that you dream are going to help us. My God! You leave your parents, you leave the rice fields, none of you for very long, and then you just go and forget all about the past."

Am told how there had been complete silence when the grave young man, who had spoken so earnestly, finished. Not a voice was raised in dissent, either from the first man, or any of the others. After that, voices murmured in discussion. While there was still some hesitancy, the first speaker spoke up once again, and three or four people supported him. Eventually it was agreed that they would each contribute a baht or two, and then they all marched off together to a newspaper office at Sao Ching Cha.

"I put in a couple of baht too," Am told Nim. "When I came out of the newspaper office, I felt different from the old Am. All my life, I never dreamed I would be of any use to anyone. But now I've become someone capable of helping my brothers in the Northeast with my own legs and my own arms."

When he came out of the printer's, Am had intended to return home, but just then, a man hailed his *samlo* and asked Am to take him across to the Thonburi side of the river. Am's passenger asked if he had been to the newspaper offices to complain about something. Am told him the story and the man had murmured, "That's the people. That's what you call the power of the people." Am had not really understood what he meant. "I felt really pleased," he continued, "to be of some use, but I was dis-couraged, too, at how few of our brothers in the Northeast the small amount of money we collected will be able to help."

The man told Am that the Peace Committee and some newspapers had, for the first consignment, collected 50,000 baht and several thousand garments, amounting to a total value of 100,000 baht. The man told him that most of the money and other contributions had come, not from wealthy and prominent people, but from the ordinary man in the street who stood on buses and trams, and lived in a small home; they had come main-ly from laborers or poor workers, from young people, women, clerks, employees, from ordinary people, both Thai and Chinese —from those whom the man had summed up as "the people."

What the man had said was all new to Am. Gazing at the morning glory shoots in his hand, he said to his wife, "They're like the morning glory I'm holding here, which Mother gathered from the canals, which grow everywhere. That's what the people are. It was like a dream, Nim, when he said that money and things for helping our brothers in the Northeast totaling 100,000 baht came from poor people, ordinary people like you and me, and not from the rich and powerful at all. People like you and me, what they call ordinary working people, the ones who create everything. I've just come to understand about the people and I'll remember it to my dying day. It's given me strength. It makes people like you, like me, like the kids, human beings of worth. And worth more, the man said, than the rich, who just scoop up the rice from our fields."

As Am took the plates over to wash, the two children who had come in to listen for a while, surrounded him and cried, "When are you going to take us to see the weapons at Sanam Luang, Daddy?" Am did not answer. When he had finished washing the plates and his hands, he wiped his mouth and hands on the edge of the *phakhama* he was wearing. The children repeated their question. As Am helped to clean up, he asked his wife, "Do you want me to take you and the children to see them showing off weapons for killing innocent people?"

Nim turned and looked at her husband in wonder.

"I don't want to see my children getting enjoyment," he continued, "out of weapons that are used for killing people. I saw the picture in the newspaper of those Koreans who were blown up by petrol bombs. I was horrified. That picture really shocked me with the cruelty of war. It made me hate war. I don't want to see a show of strength in support of war; I'd like to see a show of strength in support of peace."

"That's not your business," Nim argued. "It's the govern-ment's."

"You misunderstand. People like you and me have misunderstood for a long time. I've realized now that everything is the people's business. If the people want peace, the people can choose it. And are people like you and me going to go choosing a blasted war?"

"Where did you get these ideas from?"

"That man."

"Am, you shouldn't go repeating his words like a parrot."

"I am repeating his words, that's true. But now I'm speaking from my own awareness, because what he said was true," Am said seriously. "Just look at this business about helping our brothers in the Northeast. When the people combine their forces to help, even though they are poor, they can still provide enor-mous aid. The man said that when there were floods in the North, the people mobilized themselves to help. This was another example of the success of people power. So I believe that the power of Samson really does lie in the people, people like you and me."

"And are you going to take the children to see the foreign weapons at Sanam Luang, then?" Nim asked finally.

"He told me that it was the government's spending of the people's money, merely in preparing for war, which had brought such hardship to the people as you can see at present. If our country is really dragged into the war, it will be hell for the poor. Even in normal times they can't find solutions to the many hard-ships of the people. In time of war, the people would undoubted-ly be ignored. I would be drafted to fight, not knowing whether I was going to fight to preserve the old hardships, or what. As for you and the kids, you'd starve after that, or get robbed or buried alive under a heap of bombs."

Am shook his head. "Let's not go and get our fun from looking at those bloody weapons," he said in a loud voice. "Let's not show interest in their preparations for war. Let's you and I join the peaceniks and help restore peace, so that the people can live in happiness and peace." He turned and called his two children. "Come on, little 'uns. Get yourselves ready. I'm taking you to the zoo to see the animals and to feed them."

GLOSSARY

baht unit of Thai currency

borapet *Tinospora cordifolia (Menispermaceae)* The bitter-tasting stems were traditionally used for treating fevers, skin diseases, jaundice, and syphilis.

chao prince

chao khun pronoun or title placed before name of man of high conferred rank

chao nai member of the royal family

Hanuman the mythological monkey-king in the Thai classical epic, the *Ramakien*

Indra a Hindu deity

khun polite title used before first names

khunying pronoun or title placed before the name of a lady of high rank

mom chao prince or princess, an inherited title for the grand-children of a king

mom luang an inherited title for the great-great grandchildren of a king

mom ratchawong an inherited title for the great-grandchildren of a king

mo doctor

nai title placed before first name of a man; Mr.

nam phrik   chili sauce

phakhama   a loincloth, also used for many other purposes, including towel, child's hammock, head-cloth, etc.

Phranang Acha   a mythological princess

phra ong chao ying   princess, daughter of the king born by a lesser concubine

phraya   the second-highest rank of conferred nobility

oyasuminasai   (Jap.) good night

rai   unit of measurement (approx. 1/2 acre)

samlo   bicycle rickshaw, pedicab

Sanam Luang   a large, open expanse of land in Bangkok where official ceremonies are held

sathu   amen

soi   lane

Songkran   the name of the Thai New Year festival

wai   gesture of greeting and respect made by placing the palms of the hands together at approximately chin height

yai   grandmother; a term used for addressing and referring to elderly women

CPSIA information can be obtained at www.ICGtesting.com
Printed in the USA
LVOW07s0234260815

451478LV00034B/1958/P

9 789747 551143